ITALIAN T[...]

General Editor: KATH[...]

GIOVANNI PASCOLI: S[...]

Giovanni Pascoli

SELECTED POEMS

EDITED
WITH INTRODUCTION
NOTES AND VOCABULARY

by

P. R. HORNE, B.LITT., M.A.

MANCHESTER UNIVERSITY PRESS

Introduction, notes and all other English-language
material © Manchester University Press 1983

Published by
Manchester University Press
Oxford Road, Manchester M13 9PL

British Library cataloguing in publication data

Pascoli, Giovanni
    Selected poems.—(Italian texts)
    I. Title II. Horne, P.P. III. Series
    851'.914   PQ4835.A/

ISBN 0-7190-0870-0

Printed in Hong Kong by
Wing King Tong Co. Ltd

CONTENTS

PREFACE		ix
INTRODUCTION		1
SELECT BIBLIOGRAPHY		41
SELECTED POEMS		43

MYRICAE

1	Alba festiva	44
2	Speranze e memorie	44
3	Allora	45
4	Patria	46
5	Il nunzio	46
6	La cucitrice	47
7	Romagna	48
8	Rio Salto	50
9	I puffini dell'Adriatico	50
10	Il santuario	51
11	Tre versi dell'Ascreo	52
12	Fides	52
13	Ceppo	52
14	Orfano	53
15	Il cacciatore	53
16	Arano	54
17	Di lassú	54
18	Lavandare	55
19	La via ferrata	55
20	Mezzogiorno	56
21	Già dalla mattina	56
22	Carrettiere	56
23	In capannello	57

24	Il cane	57
25	Il mago	58
26	Contrasto	58
27	Ida e Maria	59
28	Il vecchio dei campi	60
29	Nella macchia	60
30	Dall'argine	61
31	Temporale	61
32	Dopo l'acquazzone	61
33	Pioggia	62
34	Novembre	62
35	Lo stornello	63
36	Benedizione	64
37	Con gli angioli	64
38	Mare	65
39	Il nido	65
40	Il lampo	65
41	Il tuono	66
42	La baia tranquilla	66
43	La Sirena	67

PRIMI POEMETTI

44	Il vischio	68
45	Digitale purpurea	71
46	Suor Virginia	73
47	La quercia caduta	78
48	La siepe	78
49	Nella nebbia	80
50	Il libro	81
51	Il transito	82

NUOVI POEMETTI

| 52 | La pecorella smarrita | 84 |

CANTI DI CASTELVECCHIO

| 53 | La poesia | 88 |
| 54 | Il compagno dei tagliaboschi | 91 |

55	Nebbia	93
56	Il brivido	94
57	La voce	95
58	Il sonnellino	98
59	Il gelsomino notturno	99
60	La canzone del girarrosto	100
61	L'ora di Barga	102
62	La mia sera	103
63	La servetta di monte	105
64	La cavalla storna	106
65	La tessitrice	108

POEMI CONVIVIALI
| 66 | Solon | 110 |
| 67 | Il sonno di Odisseo | 112 |

POEMI ITALICI
| 68 | Paulo Ucello | 117 |

ODI E INNI
69	A una morta	126
70	Il cane notturno	127
71	L'isola dei poeti	128
72	Inno degli emigrati italiani a Dante	130

NOTES 135
SELECT VOCABULARY 195

PREFACE

Few poets of Pascoli's stature ever had to wait so long for a balanced assessment of their poetry. Although from the first he had many enthusiastic devotees amongst the reading public at large, the road to higher critical acclaim was blocked by Croce, whose dismissive essays continued to influence critical opinion for nearly forty years. Only after the last war, and with the waning of Croce's influence, did critics begin to lose their inhibitions about appreciating the positive qualities of Pascoli's poetry; meanwhile the lengthening perspective enabled them to see that its novel features represented a new departure in the history of Italian poetry, the beginnings of modern poetic idiom. Since the centenary celebrations of 1955, which completed the reinstatement process, several good Italian anthologies have appeared, which allow the general reader to enjoy the best of Pascoli without the irritation of having to read poems that are flawed by the poet's embarrassing lack of reserve, his morbid obsessions, or any of the artistic vices condemned by Croce, in most cases with justification. Outside Italy, however, the situation is not at all satisfactory. In England Dr Purkis's pioneering anthology, published in 1938, has long been out of print, and nothing has replaced it. Moreover, the Purkis anthology itself presented only a limited conspectus of the shorter lyrics and contained nothing at all from *Poemi conviviali, Odi e Inni* or *Poemi italici.*

The present selection attempts to make good the deficiency by offering as wide a range of poems as is possible in a volume of limited proportions, chosen on the basis of quality, even though this means failing to illustrate every aspect of the poet's work. Informed readers will notice immediately the absence of some famous and much-anthologized poems, which have been judged to fall below Pascoli's best. The collections principally represented are *Myricae, Primi poemetti, Canti di Castelvecchio* and *Poemi conviviali*, since it is in these volumes that the vital Pascoli is most evident. No poems have been taken from *Poemi del Risorgimento*, because the barrier of nationality tends to make patriotic literature inaccessible to foreign readers, and no amount of study can adequately supply what, in the country of origin, is part of the national consciousness. Similar considerations apply to occasional or commemorative verse and help to explain why the *Odi e Inni* are poorly represented here, though stylistic objections can also be raised against the poems on grand public themes. In Italy commemorative poetry has traditionally required the use of a magniloquent diction which Pascoli rarely handled without artificiality. Notable exceptions are *Chavez* (among the *Odi*) and *Andrée* (one of the *Inni*), but they were left out to make room for poems with more general appeal. Individual taste has, of course, played its part in shaping the anthology, but practical considerations were also involved. Limitations of space prevent the inclusion of *Italy* (*Primi poemetti*) and of the third and best of the *Canzoni di re Enzio*, namely the *Canzone dell'olifante*. Another poem that it would be unthinkable to omit from the ideal Pascoli anthology is *Il ciocco* (*Canti di Castelvecchio*), but as well as being very long, it contains linguistic difficulties that make it unsuitable for a volume which may be read by students of Italian in school.

The first half of the Introduction is biographical; the second half is devoted exclusively to illustrating Pascoli's poetic innovations, in order that readers having only a limited acquaintance with Italian poetry may better understand why Pascoli is such an important landmark. Readers wishing to study in greater detail the technical matters of metre and versification which are discussed should consult W. T. Elwert's *Versificazione italiana*, a translation of the original German work *Italienische Metrik*, and G. L. Beccaria's *Metrica e sintassi nella poesia di Giovanni Pascoli*. General studies of Pascoli's poetry are legion, and the titles of some of the more useful ones appear in the bibliography.

The Vocabulary has been compiled on the assumption that the reader is familiar with the 2200 words listed in *Italiano fondamentale* by Maria and Dennis Riddiford and Terence Best, whilst the Notes aim chiefly at removing the linguistic and other difficulties that stand in the way of a clear understanding of the literal sense. It may be true, as T. S. Eliot observed in connection with Dante, that 'genuine poetry can communicate before it is understood', but imperfect understanding is a poor foundation on which to base interpretations and evaluations. Discerning readers will, it is hoped, welcome an editorial approach which offers the texts without subjective 'appreciations' in the belief that the poems themselves are the clearest statement of what poetry is and need no further recommendation.

My best thanks go to Dr J. R. Woodhouse for criticizing an early draft of the Introduction and Notes, to Dr V. Lucchesi for helping to resolve some linguistic problems, to P. T. Eden for his critical proof-reading and to Dr Kathleen Speight for her encouragement and advice at every stage of the book's preparation.

P.R.H.

INTRODUCTION

I

The poet was born on the last day of December 1855 at San Mauro, now called San Mauro Pascoli, in Romagna. The house in which he was born — 'quella casa bianca con le persiane verdi' — is remembered with many of its characteristic features in *Casa mia* and other poems; it was in the garden here that he fought the mock battles with his brothers described in one of his prose memoirs. His elementary school, at Savignano-sul-Rubicone, was a little more than a mile away in one direction; four miles away in the opposite direction, on the Adriatic coast, lay Bellaria, the destination for summer beach excursions; ten miles to the south one could just make out the faint outline of San Marino on its hilltop: 'l'azzurra visïon di San Marino' as described in the poem *Romagna*. Apart from the house at San Mauro, the other centre of Pascoli's life during early childhood was the Torlonia estate at Torre di San Mauro which his father managed. Indeed, for the last five years of his father's life (1862—7) the family lived permanently in a house belonging to the estate, though for most of this time the future poet was at his boarding-school in Urbino. A photograph of the Torlonia villa in Maria Pascoli's biography of her brother shows the stream called the Rio Salto running down one boundary of the estate and the line of poplars along the bank which Pascoli mentions in his poem of this name. These were some of the landmarks of that 'ideal world' of the poet's imagination alluded to in a letter that he wrote following a visit to the region in later life (1897): 'il mio mondo ideale . . . che ha per confini il Luso e il Rio Salto, e per centri la chiesuola della Madonna dell'Acqua e il camposanto fosco di cipressi.' The Uso — Pascoli's 'Luso' — is a stream which flows near San Mauro down to the sea at Bellaria. In this corner of Romagna he laid up during his boyhood the store of impressions on which he was to draw for many of the poems that found their way into the collection *Myricae* and into the section of *Canti di Castelvecchio* entitled 'Ritorno a San Mauro'. The impressions were still vivid in 1911 when he described, with the precision of vocabulary typical of so much of his poetry, the sights and sounds which had surrounded him in his youth:

... lo squillar dei magli sulle incudini e il tonfar dei martelli sul cuoio e il ronfar delle seghe nel legno e il cantar del garzuolo tra i raffi, e ... tutto l'assiduo rumore di calcole e pettini e il vario tramestío delle faccende casereccie e anche il frullar de' fusi e il tenue tintinno de' ferri da calze ...

The enumeration continues with references to outdoor activities in the fields: oxen ploughing, long lines of reapers, and the corn harvest, when the harvesters 'abbicano in alti monumenti nereggianti poi a notte tra lo sfavillío delle lucciole, i covoni del grano'.

The idyllic picture evoked by these words contrasts sharply with the violent reality of life in the Romagna of Pascoli's childhood, and it was this reality, breaking in on the hitherto secure world of family life, that gave the boy his first experience of injustice. On 10 August 1867 — the date remained an obsession with the poet for the rest of his life — Ruggero Pascoli, his father, was killed by a gun-shot wound in the head as he was returning from Cesena alone in his brake drawn by the grey mare of the poem *La cavalla storna*. It seems that the murder had been carefully planned and was not one of those casual acts of aggression, reports of which appeared frequently in the newspapers of the time. Some six or seven years after the event the poet and his brother Raffaele started strenuous enquiries in the localities of San Mauro and Savignano, hoping to find some evidence to support their suspicions about the instigator of the crime, but the investigations met only with hostility, with threats of reprisal against their brother Giacomo's family and, on one occasion, with actual physical violence to themselves. There was a vein of stubbornness and belligerence in the character of the poet, whose sense of outrage was never assuaged. In his eyes a double injustice had been committed. A man universally respected for his fairness and rectitude had been cut off in the prime of his life:

>dissero, oh! sí! dissero ch'era sano,
>e che avrebbe vissuto anche molti anni.
>Ma uno squarcio aveva egli nel capo,
>ma piena del suo sangue era una mano.
>
>(*Canti di Castelvecchio: Un ricordo*, 85–8)

Furthermore the police, either through dilatoriness or for a more culpable reason, had failed to bring the guilty to justice. Pascoli had no doubts about the identity of the man of influence who had instigated the killing and who was so strangely immune from prosecution. Every year, on 10 August, he received from the poet a note to remind him of the anniversary.

A second and crucial phase of the poet's social and political education opened at Bologna in the autumn of 1873 when, having won a scholarship to the university, he enrolled as a student in the Faculty of Letters under Carducci. In the year following his matriculation there took place in the region of Bologna an abortive popular uprising instigated by the Russian anarchist Bakunin and directed locally by the charismatic Andrea Costa, shortly to become Pascoli's friend and destined subsequently to be the first Socialist deputy in the Italian parliament. The insurrection of 1874, which the police were able to suppress before the agitators had even achieved their first objective, was one of a series of disturbances up and down the peninsula which reflect the climate of popular discontent in which the young Italian parliament was attempting to carry out the political consolidation of the state. It must be remembered that the kingdom had been constituted as recently as 1860 (at the time of Pascoli's birth San Mauro was still a papal possession like the rest of the region of Emilia-Romagna) and that the unification of Italy had not been completed until a decade later, with the addition of the Veneto. Paradoxically, during the first twenty-five years of the nation's life, government policies actually tended to increase rather than reduce the tensions and divisions (both geographical and social) that had existed before the unification. Large sums of money were needed to build up the military and administrative paraphernalia of a modern nation-state and to lay the foundations of Italy's future industrial economy through public works and subsidies. The burden of the taxation necessary to finance these programmes fell disproportionately on areas like Emilia where the economy was predominantly agricultural. Thus it was that during the first quarter-century of the nation's existence the voices of discontent were loudest in the rural areas of the peninsula (and loudest of all in the south). It was this discontent which the anarchists, headed by Costa, sought to channel into direct action, convinced that the moment had arrived for the 'liquidation of the bourgeois capitalist state'. In these conditions the socialist movement came into being in Italy.

The student Pascoli had shown early on his sympathy with the cause of the political agitators by contributing to their publications, but it was through Costa, whom he met towards the end of 1876, shortly after Costa's trial and triumphant acquittal, that he became really active in the socialist cause, joining the local branch of the communist organization, the *Associazione internazionale dei lavoratori*. As an *internazionalista* he addressed Association meetings in Bologna and elsewhere, distributed its literature and — after the banning of the Association in 1877 — helped to reorganize it in secret with the assistance of his contemporary and greatest friend at Bologna, Severino Ferrari, another of Carducci's famous pupils. The militant phase of Pascoli's socialism ended in 1879 with his arrest on a charge of incitement to violence arising out of an episode shortly to be recounted. Although the charge was dismissed when the case eventually came to court, Pascoli had by then suffered the rigours of two and a half months of preventive detention in gaol (7 September to 22 December).

The prison experience in no way diminished Pascoli's support for the ultimate objectives of his former revolutionary associates, but it precipitated a break between himself and the activists of the socialist movement that was inevitable in view of his abhorrence of violence, evidenced by his angry reaction to the attempted assassination of King Umberto in November 1878: 'Non si deve uccidere; la vita è sacra, a chiunque appartenga, e deve essere sempre rispettata da tutti.' However, this repudiation of violence as a means of furthering political aims did not prevent Pascoli from attending the trial of the *internazionalisti* arrested for demonstrating against the conviction of the would-be assassin, Passanante. In the courtroom, after sentence had been passed, he voiced publicly his sympathy for the activists with the words: 'Se questi sono i malfattori, evviva i malfattori!' On his way home from attending the trial Pascoli was detained by the police (7 September 1879) and interrogated. Among his answers to the police interrogator is the following statement about his political allegiances:

Non appartengo ad alcun partito politico ... Le mie idee mi conducono ad appartenere a quella parte di socialisti che desiderano il miglioramento della società senza pervertimento dell'ordine, e ad ammirare la generosità di chi si sacrifica per studiare il mezzo di raggiungere tale miglioramento.

The four years leading up to his arrest and detainment in prison taxed to the limit Pascoli's powers of physical and mental endurance. His troubles had begun in the autumn of

1875, when, to punish him for taking part in a student demonstration, the authorities stopped his scholarship and took his name off the academic register. Without the scholarship and with no parents to turn to for subvention, even the bare necessities of life were hard to come by. In addition, Pascoli's life was saddened by the death in 1876 of his brother, Giacomo, only recently married, who left behind in the house at San Mauro a young widow and a baby son. The poem *La voce*, which recalls this difficult period of the poet's life, suggests that his mind was often filled with nostalgic memories of his parents (his mother had survived Ruggero Pascoli's death by only a year) and of the five brothers and sisters who had been struck down by illness at a premature age and who now lay in the 'cypress-dark' cemetery half way between San Mauro and Savignano. Of the once numerous family there now remained only Giovanni himself, his two younger brothers Raffaele and Giuseppe, and the 'pie sorelline in convento': Ida and Maria. However, San Mauro had more than just sad memories to offer, for it was here on one of his holiday visits that Pascoli had become acquainted with Erminia Tognacci (see *La tessitrice*); but even this solace was brief, for she died of tuberculosis in April 1878 at the early age of twenty. At long last, during the academic year 1879/80, Pascoli's scholarship was restored, and he was able to graduate in the summer of 1882. By now he was twenty-seven years of age, conscious of his position as head of the family and of his responsibilities towards Ida (aged nineteen) and Maria (aged seventeen) in the convent-school run by the Augustinian nuns at Sogliano, where their aunt Rita was keeping an eye on them.

Pascoli was launched on his professional career as a classics teacher on 21 September 1882. As is normal on the continent, where many teachers destined for university posts start out as school-teachers, Pascoli's first teaching appointments were in secondary schools: initially at the Liceo Duni in Matera (in the province of Cosenza) as head teacher in Latin and Greek, then at *licei* in Massa (1884—7) and Livorno, where he remained until 1895. His teaching day was a long one, for he was compelled to augment his inadequate salary by undertaking additional teaching; the consequent drain on his time and energy meant at first a curtailment of his poetic activities compared with the days at Bologna where his output of occasional verse had been quite copious. At Matera he was unable to realize any of his poetic projects, one of which — outlined in a letter to Severino Ferrari dated 9 January 1883 — affords a first glimpse of the sort of poem that was to predominate in the collection entitled *Myricae*:

Io ho intravisto certi canti! una serie di pístole [= *epistole*] e pistolotti; i pistolotti di quattro strofe l'uno: tanti quadretti naturali, voci de' boschi e delle strade; le pístole in quartine, stile mezzano; voli affettuosi senza ricercatezza, un certo risolino diffuso.

Pascoli's brief comment on the style he intended for his projected poems (*stile mezzano . . . senza ricercatezza*) points to the area in which he hoped to establish the originality of his own poetic voice alongside his already famous contemporaries: a style less solemn than Carducci's, less recherché than that of d'Annunzio and his imitators. 'Studio Orazio' — the letter to Ferrari continues — 'Vorrei distinguermi da codesti poeti cromolitografici incipriati alla d'Annunzio'.

The poetically barren years ended after Pascoli's transfer to Massa. Not that the demands of the job were diminished, but the Tuscan landscape and the Tuscan language acted as powerful stimuli and released new energies in the poet. At Massa he completed the group of poems that figure in the section of *Myricae* entitled 'L'ultima passeggiata', and under this latter title they appeared in print in 1886. The first edition proper of *Myricae* (containing 22 poems) was published privately in 1891 in honour of the wedding of Pascoli's friend Raffaello Marcovigi. A commercial edition (72 poems) appeared in 1892 and was followed by an enlarged edition (116 poems) in 1894. All these early editions of *Myricae*, up to and including the sixth and definitive edition of 1903 containing over 150 poems, were published by Giusti at Livorno. By and large the Livorno years were astonishingly productive for the poet, considering the extent of his teaching commitments. In addition to the *Myricae*, his output of Italian poetry included the earliest of the *Poemetti*, for which Tuscany supplied both the linguistic and the descriptive *ambiente*. He also completed the first of the *Poemi conviviali* and sent them to Adolfo De Bosis at Rome for publication in his twelve-part symposium of Italian art and letters called *Il Convito*: hence the title chosen by Pascoli for his collection. Other original compositions were the Latin poems which, at regular intervals from 1892 onwards, he submitted to the Academy of Sciences in

Amsterdam as contenders for the annual Hoeufft prize. With equal regularity they were awarded the first prize of the gold medallion: after *Veianius* (1892) came *Phidyle* (1894), followed by *Myrmedon* in 1895, and the list could be continued for subsequent years. During the same three years he completed *Lyra Romana* (an anthology of Latin lyric poetry for schools) and worked on *Epos* (a companion volume containing selections of epic poetry). Meanwhile his first essays on Dante (*Minerva oscura*) were, like the early *Poemi conviviali*, appearing in successive volumes of *Il Convito*. Despite this considerable output Pascoli complained constantly that his teaching duties made it impossible for him to function properly as a writer. By 1894 the physical strain and mental frustration had become so unbearable that he requested — and was granted — temporary leave of absence from school for the scholastic year 1894/5. But his hopes of enjoying an uninterrupted spell of activity devoted entirely to his own poetry were dashed when his sister Ida announced her intention of getting married. Pascoli reacted to the news like a man who had been sentenced to death.

To understand why the poet was so distressed by an event that in most families would be regarded as normal, desirable and fairly predictable, it is necessary to go back to the year of his arrival at Massa and consider the relationship between the poet and his two sisters. Ever since Pascoli's graduation in 1882 he had looked forward to the time when he would be able to provide a home for the two girls, to whom he felt attached by an almost paternal bond of affection. When the reunion at last became possible — in May 1885 — the poet was in his thirtieth year, the elder sister was twenty-two and the younger twenty. Moving on another five years, we find the close-knit little group still together, ensconced in their house at Livorno and enjoying somewhat easier financial circumstances. Ida is in charge of the household and is affectionately known as 'la Reginella' by the other two. Maria has become the poet's *confidante*. It is she who sits with him in his study while he works; she who copies out for him the prayers which they say together every evening, so that when he has to stay nights away from home (a rare event and an unpleasant one for the poet, so great is his attachment to the domestic intimacy of his family circle) he can recite them in his hotel bedroom and feel united again with his sisters in spirit. Such devout behaviour in a man who was not a practising Catholic is illuminating: it reveals, on the one hand, the acute sense of isolation that he experienced when separated from the rest of the trio, on the other the power of the nostalgic attraction exerted on the poet's emotions by a religion which did not command his intellectual assent. Much has been written about Pascoli's religious sentiments, largely because the poet himself had no clear-cut convictions. The problem of religious faith was one that he could not resolve one way or the other. He longed for the feeling of security that belief in a transcendent reality might have brought, but the climate of scientific positivism in which he grew up, coupled with his natural tendency to indecision, kept him in a chronic state of suspension between agnosticism and belief. With regard specifically to Christianity, he accepted its ethic, but was indifferent to Catholic dogma and maintained an attitude approaching hostility towards the institution of the Church and — with some exceptions — its ministers.

When the blow fell, and Ida gave notice of the decision that would break up the household after a decade of fraternal solidarity, Pascoli was temporarily disorientated. He was in Rome at this time, seconded to the Ministry of Education (a condition of his leave of absence from Livorno); consequently there is ample documentation of his state of mind in the copious correspondence that he maintained with his sisters. Two themes recur in these letters: the ingratitude of Ida, whom he regards as a deserter from the family nest which he had been at such pains to build; and the intolerable future ahead for Maria and himself, condemned to witness the matrimonial joys of their sister whilst themselves being excluded from them. The hypersensitivity of the poet is everywhere apparent in these overexcited outpourings of bitterness, irritation and envy. Nor did the verbal expression of his feelings bring sufficient relief. Within a year of Ida's betrothal he himself was engaged to be married to his cousin Imelde Morri, though the engagement was as shortlived as it was precipitate. Maria, who had been kept ignorant of the development and found out merely by chance, was resentful that her brother had not consulted her before taking such a serious step, and her hostile attitude at this juncture was decisive in bringing about an immediate rupture between the poet and his fiancée.

This domestic drama, which reveals so clearly the emotional

intensity of the relations between the poet and his sisters, and the mutual dependence of Maria and her brother, marked the end of the poet's aspirations to marriage. There had been other occasions on which he had thought of taking a wife, but it would appear that his emotions had not been deeply committed either to Giulietta Poggi (in 1883) or to Lia Bianchi (in 1889). His own comment, many years later, on the fact that he had never married is a humorous one: when asked to name his ruling passion, he replied lightheartedly: 'Sarebbe l'amore: è . . . il fumo.' With smoking he might have coupled his love of wine, which earned him his reputation for conviviality (and worse).

At Rome in the summer of 1895 Pascoli was introduced by Adolfo De Bosis to another famous contributor to *Il Convito*, Gabriele d'Annunzio. This was the first time that the two poets had met, though they had corresponded since 1893. They were attentive and appreciative readers of each other's works and recognized that, however different their personal life-styles, they were ploughing parallel furrows in the field of poetry. On receiving a copy of some sonnets which Pascoli had published in celebration of his brother Raffaele's wedding, d'Annunzio at once wrote a complimentary review for *La Tribuna* (Rome, 7 April 1888), praising their elegant craftsmanship and the 'liveliness and freshness of the language'. The 1892 edition of *Myricae* was reviewed by d'Annunzio in even more glowing terms (*Il Mattino*, Naples, 30-1 December 1892), though his general enthusiasm did not prevent him from criticizing Pascoli's choice vocabulary for its occasional lack of spontaneity. The reviewer would also have liked more musicality, more mystery: an interesting criticism in view of the way that these areas came to be explored later on in *Canti di Castelvecchio*. The review of 1892 is remarkable for the number of facets that d'Annunzio succeeded in identifying at a first reading of *Myricae*. He again makes a point of praising Pascoli's mastery of Italian metres and hails him as the only contemporary poet who has successfully revived old traditional verse-forms, infusing them with new life and modern sentiments. Twelve years later d'Annunzio was to give an enthusiastic reception to *Poemi conviviali*: 'Non mi ricordo di aver avuto tanta ebrezza da alcun altro libro di poesia' (Letter to Pascoli dated 7 September 1904).

Pascoli's attitude towards d'Annunzio was complicated by

his aversion to d'Annunzio's aristocratic, flamboyant way of life and by a sense of inferiority stemming from the recognition that he was in debt to his younger and more famous contemporary for giving him some favourable publicity. These temperamental reactions on Pascoli's side helped to bring about a brief period of estrangement between 1900 and 1903; but as regards d'Annunzio's poetry the older man had considerable admiration for the writer he addressed as his 'brother': 'fratello minor d'anni e maggiore di meriti' (letter dated 5 September 1903); 'O mio fratello, minore e maggiore, Gabriele!' (Preface to *Poemi conviviali*).

By the summer of 1895 the prospects for Pascoli's future career had begun to look brighter, for in August he was notified by the Education Minister that he was being considered for a university post, perhaps at Turin. Departure from Livorno being now imminent, the search began for a house to suit the needs of the new ménage, shortly to be reduced to two. By a lucky chance the ideal place was brought to the poet's notice in the very month of Ida's wedding (September 1895). It was at Castelvecchio in the Tuscan commune of Barga (eight miles from Bagni di Lucca), which at this time, before the building of the branch railway, was a good deal more remote than it is today, it being a five-hour carriage drive from Lucca to Barga. The Pascoli house looked out across the valley of the Serchio towards Monte Pania and the Apuan Alps. The top storey at the front consisted of a verandah or loggia (the *altana* of *Il libro*), whilst the back overlooked the large orchard alluded to in *Il vischio*. The country setting and magnificent views were peculiarly congenial to the poet, who wrote many of his finest lyrics with this setting in mind: poems that appeared in *Poemetti* (first edition 1897) and of course in *Canti di Castelvecchio* (first edition 1903). The house, which he was eventually in a position to buy, partly by the sale of his gold medallions from Amsterdam, was to be his permanent residence for the rest of his life. Here he spent vacations, transferring himself to the university during term-time and as his duties required.

The university appointment, when it came through, was not for Turin as had been expected, but for Bologna, where Pascoli delivered his inaugural lecture on 21 January 1896. In more favourable circumstances this return to the scenes of his early manhood to work alongside colleagues like his old friend Severino Ferrari and some of his former teachers would have been a source of pleasure and satisfaction. But Pascoli found the terms of his appointment as a teacher of classical philology too narrow for his liking. Also there were family circumstances which made Bologna an impossible place for the time being, namely the close proximity of brother Giuseppe, whose irregular way of life and sponging habits profoundly offended the poet and his sister. Accordingly, when Giuseppe moved to Bologna in January 1897, Pascoli at once resigned his post; but this setback to his academic career was only brief, and by the start of the next academic year (1897/98) he was already installing himself in a new post: at Messina university this time, as Professor of Latin literature.

The Bologna years had seen the maturing of Pascoli's views concerning the nature and function of poetry and the composition of his famous essay *Il fanciullino* (1897). In a way this was a by-product of the Leopardi studies on which he had earlier been engaged preparatory to a public lecture on *Il sabato del villaggio* (given in Florence in 1896) and which helped to crystallize his ideas about the *raison d'être* of his own poetry. The essay owes its title to the notion of the 'eternal child' in all of us, which Pascoli borrowed from a passage in Plato's *Phaedo*. He thinks of the poet as looking out on the world with the innocent gaze of a child, perceiving without making moral judgments and without imposing intellectual interpretations on what he perceives. This childlike, or naive, or ingenuous vision, implying as it does the immediate apprehension of reality without the participation of the critical faculties of the rational mind, is akin to what, in the philosophical language of Croce's aesthetics, is termed 'intuition', only Pascoli calls it by a more homely name: 'un modo fanciullesco [di ragionare] che si chiama profondo, perché d'un tratto, senza farci scendere a uno a uno i gradini del pensiero, ci trasporta nell'abisso della verità' (Section IV, p. 14).[1] By virtue of this distinctive way of seeing things, poetry — in common with other forms of art — is an autonomous activity. 'Il poeta è poeta, non oratore o predicatore, non filosofo, non istorico, non maestro, non tribuno o demagogo, non uomo di stato o di corte' (Section XI, p. 31). Nor is the poet 'merely' a craftsman: 'E nemmeno è ... un artista che nielli e ceselli l'oro che altri gli porga' (*ibid.*). Furthermore, since there is only one kind of vision which is genuinely poetic, poetry is one whatever its theme, scope or style, and distinctions such as Romantic, Classical and so on are unreal and unjustified: 'E quindi, né c'è poesia arcadica, romantica, classica, né poesia italiana, greca, sanscrita; ma poesia soltanto, soltanto poesia, e... non poesia' (Section XII, p. 36). These last few quotations might easily be mistaken for excerpts from Croce's *Breviario di estetica*; to Pascoli's annoyance, however, the philosopher never deigned to acknowledge his essay, although it preceded by five years the first edition of Croce's *Estetica* (1902) and by more than a decade the *Breviario* (1913).

In asserting that art is an autonomous form of intellectual activity distinct from other intellectual activities, Pascoli was not implying that the spheres of art and life are separate and unrelated. The poetic process may be *sui generis*, but the individual poetic work is rooted in the poet's general experience of life. This is affirmed at every turn by what Pascoli says about the poet's method of working and about the moral and social usefulness of his poems. The true poet, he maintains, is not an inventor, but a discoverer: his task is to discover the new in the familiar and to uncover the essence of things under their outward appearances: 'Poesia è trovare nelle cose, come ho a dire?, il loro sorriso e la loro lacrima' (Section VIII, p. 22). The combination of novelty with familiarity is important. What the poet 'discovers' may have the appearance of novelty, but his readers will instantly recognize the truth of what he reveals to them: 'Il poeta è colui che esprime la parola che tutti avevano sulle labbra e che nessuno avrebbe detta' (Section XI, p. 32). The impression of novelty does not depend on stylistic artifice (on the contrary, 'Lo studio deve togliere gli artifizi e renderci la natura' (Section XIII, p. 41)), nor is it a matter of fantastic invention: 'Il nuovo non s'inventa: si scopre' (Section VI, p. 18). Rather is it the peculiar power of the poetic vision to see what was always there, but was overlooked: 'nelle cose è il nuovo, per chi sa vederlo' (*ibid*.). It is a matter of helping people to see what previously they had ignored, to see things as though for the first time as they really are, and the impression of novelty arises from the shock of this revelation. To achieve his goal the poet must have at his disposal a language rich in words capable of evoking things in all their individuality and specificness (Section XIV). In the view of many critics this attention to the world of objects and to the power of the word to evoke the object — what has come to be termed *la poetica degli oggetti* — is the most important aspect of the *Fanciullino* essay. There will be another reference to it in the second part of this introduction.

A second prominent cluster of ideas relates to the function of poetry, whose moral and social usefulness is asserted several times in the course of the essay. Pascoli tends to be dogmatic on this matter, and the supporting argument is correspondingly thin. In part he relies on restating an earlier Romantic belief in the indivisibility of the True, the Good and the Beautiful, according to which the immoral is intrinsically unpoetic. His only original contribution to the argument is the suggestion that poetry of the right kind (that is, *his* kind) may help to reduce social strife by persuading people to find satisfaction and contentment in what is immediately to hand, instead of indulging in the reckless pursuit of their egotistical desires: 'intenso il sentimento poetico è di chi trova la poesia in ciò che lo circonda . . . E sommamente benefico è tale sentimento, che pone un soave e leggero freno all' instancabile desiderio' (Section VIII, p. 23). The same point was to be made more succinctly by Pascoli in the preface to his anthology *Sul limitare* (1902); '[La poesia] è una gran cosa, perché è quella che fa che noi ci *contentiamo*' (his own italics).

The basic idea of the *Fanciullino* — the notion of the ingenuousness of true poetic vision — still occupied Pascoli's mind when he wrote the preface to *Nuovi poemetti* in 1909. Here, as in the earlier preface to *Odi e Inni* (1906), he addresses himself to an ideal audience of *anime giovanili*, in the belief that only the young, or those who have managed to preserve a youthful receptiveness and openness of mind, can give to poetry the sympathetic attention that it requires if it is to be properly understood. It would be reasonable, therefore, to attempt to relate his theories of poetry to any of the poems which he thought of as constituting the first phase of his poetic activity, including the *Odi e Inni*; in fact, however, the poetics of the *Fanciullino* apply only to one part — albeit a large one — of Pascoli's output: to *Myricae*, *Canti di Castelvecchio* and the two volumes of *Poemetti*.[2]

Pascoli's time in Sicily, which lasted until 1902, was one of the happiest and most fruitful periods of his life, his imagination being stimulated alike by the Sicilian landscape and by the island's classical past. The relatively large number of poems in our selection dating from these years is a reflection of their poetic productiveness. At the same time the poet was active in other areas of literary and scholarly endeavour, devoting much time and energy on the one hand to his Dante studies and on the other to a series of public addresses in which he voiced his moral and political views. Some of these papers or talks, which are to be found in the section of Pascoli's prose works entitled *Pensieri e Discorsi*, were a direct response to the political, social and economic turmoil of this period.

The poet's arrival in Messina coincided with a specially difficult time in the economic and social life of Italy, which passed through a decade of crisis at the end of the century. Spectacular symptoms of the malaise affecting industry and commerce were the liquidation of the *Banca romana* and the failure soon afterwards of the *Credito mobiliare* and the *Banca generale*, all in the years 1893—4. Meanwhile a series of disastrous harvests brought penury to those who depended for their livelihood on the land. The privations suffered by wage-earners in general led to serious public disorder: there were riots in Sicily in 1893—4, and similar scenes were re-enacted in 1898 in Rome, Milan and elsewhere. At the height of the troubles in this year martial law was in force in many provinces. In a passionate poem entitled *Pace!* (1898) Pascoli appealed to the two sides in the conflict, workers and employers, to come together and settle their differences. Given the economic conditions prevailing during this period, it is hardly surprising that militant socialism made rapid progress: there were five Socialists (including Andrea Costa) in parliament in 1892, the year in which the Italian Socialist party was founded; by 1897 Socialist representation had risen to twenty seats, and by 1900 to thirty-two seats out of five hundred. However, the pressure exerted by Socialist deputies in parliament was insufficient to influence the policies of an inept government. Public violence increased, and as the century drew to a close, it appeared doubtful whether the constitution would survive the tensions created by the high-handed intransigence of the extreme Right and the hostility of the extreme Left in opposition. The assassination of King Umberto in 1900 (an event commemorated by Pascoli in his ode *Al re Umberto*) looked like another step on the road to revolution. If the constitution was saved for the time being, it was due to two circumstances: the emergence as Premier of a moderate statesman, Giovanni Giolitti, with the ability to operate a liberal parliamentary dictatorship within the old system of transformism; and a period of rapid industrial expansion and economic growth that lasted up to the outbreak of World War I. This period of national prosperity alleviated one of the root causes of social unrest, so reducing the pressure from the extreme Left and reassuring the more fearful members of the ruling class, who could now permit themselves to become less intolerant of change. A sustained period of liberal reform was at last possible.

Such was the background to Pascoli's *Discorsi* of his Sicilian period, three of which are especially important for understanding the nature of the poet's convictions at this stage of his life: *L'era nuova* of 1899, which deals with the mission of poets in a scientific age; the Garibaldi commemoration of 2 June 1901 entitled *L'eroe italico*; and lastly *L'avvento* (December 1901), which is the fullest public statement that we have of Pascoli's views about contemporary society and politics.

The *Discorsi* all have a high moral tone, whatever their theme or occasion. Thus the mission of the poet outlined in *L'era nuova* is regarded as essentially a moral one, in keeping with Pascoli's earlier statements on the subject in *Il fanciullino*. In answer to the question: 'What is the function of the poet and of poetry in a scientific age?', Pascoli replies, using a play on words for which there is no English equivalent: 'il poeta è quello e la poesia è ciò che della scienza fa coscienza'. *Scienza* in this context means 'scientific knowledge' rather than knowledge in general; more specifically, Pascoli alludes to the knowledge that mankind is an infinitesimally small part of the macrocosm. *Coscienza* means both 'conscience' and 'consciousness'. So the poet acts as a mediator, interpreting the findings of science for the benefit of the common man. He reminds the reader of the realities of the human condition, presenting them in such a light that they become more than just parts of the reader's intellectual baggage and actually modify his behaviour; scientific knowledge (*scienza*) is turned into moral awareness (*coscienza*). In the long term, says Pascoli, if the universal brotherhood of man ever becomes an historical reality, it will have been due largely to the humanizing influence of poetry, which teaches men the absurdity of internecine strife. This message recalls the conclusion of an earlier paper of 1898 devoted to Leopardi's great poem *La ginestra*, which Pascoli interprets as an exhortation to peace and mutual cooperation as being the only hope for man's survival in a universe governed by destructive natural forces. Even in the most self-consciously 'political' of the *Discorsi* — *Una sagra*, delivered during the election campaign of June 1900 — it is brotherly love, not the desire for justice or social progress, which is stated to be the mainspring of political action.

It is easy to recognize, in the author of the *Discorsi*, the idealist who in his student days had been a member of the Communist International. Pascoli in middle age retains his old concern for the victims of social oppression, preserves his idealistic faith in a future when all men will be truly brothers and all conflicts have been resolved. But in other respects he has changed. The distrust of political factions and party creeds which he voiced to the police in 1879 is stronger now, and perhaps more justified considering the unedifying conduct of the Italian parliament in the interim; young people are now urged by him to shun political parties because they stifle freedom of thought and conscience: 'Altro è avere idee, altro, essere d'un partito' (*L'eroe italico*, p. 206). In addition, a completely new facet of Pascoli's outlook compared with twenty years previously is the importance which he now attaches to nationalism. The label that he himself coined to describe his political credo in *Una sagra* was 'socialismo patriottico', and in the Garibaldi commemoration of the following year the patriotic or nationalistic strand of his thought was especially apparent. In part this was due to the occasion of the address (a celebration of Italy's most popular national hero), but it was also a response to the contemporary trend in world politics towards imperialism, as instanced by the British involvement in South Africa. Smaller nations like Italy must be prepared to protect the integrity of their frontiers, by force of arms if necessary.

The ethical content of Pascoli's 'patriotic socialism' is clearly evident in the second *discorso* of 1901, which he delivered during the Advent season, just before Christmas. The title of the address — *L'avvento* — is a pun, for Pascoli salutes not only the approaching Christian feast of the nativity, but also the commencement of a new phase of evolution in the history of mankind. This is the emergence of what he chooses to call *homo humanus*, who is *homo sapiens* at a later stage of evolution. (The post-Darwinian way of thinking about social development is reminiscent of Fogazzaro's theory of *ascensioni umane*, which Pascoli mentions.) The new breed of men is characterized by compassion (*pietà*), in the exercise of which they perform acts of altruism that contradict the promptings of instinct and intelligence. Evidence that the age of *homo humanus* has dawned is the rise of socialism: 'Il socialismo! Senz'altri argomenti e fatti, basterebbe questo, del sorgere del socialismo, a dimostrare che il regno della pietà è già inoltrato. Esso è un fenomeno d'altruismo' (p. 223). Whatever may have been the case in his student days — and there is no evidence that even then it had a reasoned ideological basis — Pascoli's socialism at this later period of his life is devoid of political content and is more a moral than a political sentiment; 'religion' is the word that he himself applied to his beliefs in a letter written at about this time to his friend Alfredo Caselli. He claims, at the end of *L'avvento*, that he has not turned his back on the political activists with whom he worked in his youth, and in spirit he has not. He still shares their sense of outrage at the effects of injustice and oppression, but does not believe that economic and social theorizing can help to mitigate them. (In the same letter to Caselli of 14 January 1901 he refers specifically to Marxist theory as the 'da me odiato sempre ... credo Marxistico'.) Justice has become for him less important than compassion, and political programmes of less consequence than the individual's moral obligations towards his fellow men. In short, Pascoli's 'patriotic socialism' is not so much socialism as humanitarianism, which continues to subsist awkwardly alongside an outlook increasingly antidemocratic and élitist.

The nationalistic sentiments expressed in the Messina *Discorsi* found an answering echo in the fresh cultural environment in which Pascoli found himself when, in 1903, he took up a new post as Professor of classical languages at Pisa university. One of his new acquaintances was Enrico Corradini, founder of the Florentine periodical *Il Regno*, which was a platform for Prezzolini, Papini and other, less moderate prophets of a new age of Italian power and expansion. In his reply to a survey conducted by the magazine in 1904 to test the extent of public support for the so-called 'Triple Alliance' (Italy, Germany, Austria), Pascoli, who was against the *Triplice*, sketched the idea of a Pan-Latin federation promoted by a resurgent Italian nation united within her natural boundaries. A sizeable wedge of territory comprising the modern region of Trentino-Alto Adige still belonged to Austria; together with

Trieste it was the object of fervent irredentist aspirations of the kind that Pascoli robustly voiced in his reply to the *inchiesta*: 'È ora di riprendere l'opera eroica, . . . di riconquistare l'Italia all'Italia.' He maintained this position for the rest of his life and applauded the government's decision when — in response to a wave of strident jingoism — it embarked on the colonial conquest of Libya in 1911.

The Pisan period was important because of the tireless energy with which Pascoli worked to complete, for the Bolognese publisher Zanichelli, a uniform definitive edition of all his existing poetry, being impatient to initiate a new cycle of poetic activity which he believed would surpass everything he had so far written. 'Ho fretta di liquidare la mia vecchia opera poetica per cominciare la nuova' he wrote to Vittorio Cian on 31 July 1904, a few weeks before the publication of the *Poemi conviviali* ('la mia cosa migliore'), and this was followed later the same year by a revised and reconstituted edition of the *poemetti*. Some new compositions were added, some older ones removed, with the aim of producing a collection more faithful overall to the spirit of the earliest poems in the volume. The new title — *Primi poemetti* — reflected this change as well as looking forward to a second volume, *Nuovi poemetti*, which was forthcoming in 1909. Meanwhile the bulk of the *Odi e Inni* passed from conception to completion, and the work was published in 1906. Although Pascoli himself regarded the *Odi e Inni* as an aspect of his 'old' poetry, their heroic style may be seen as in some sense marking a transition to the 'new' manner of treating in heroic or epic style subjects from Italian history (*Poemi del Risorgimento, Le canzoni di re Enzio*). Posterity has not endorsed Pascoli's own view of this last phase of poetic activity as being his finest, and modern critical opinion is more inclined to regard the best of Pascoli as being contained in the first six volumes of his poetic output, the final systemization of which dates from the serene stock-taking period at Pisa.

This happy period would have lasted longer if it had not been for the retirement of Giosuè Carducci at Bologna, which left vacant the most celebrated Chair of Letters in the whole of Italy. Pascoli's hesitation in accepting the appointment offered to him was typical of his irresolute nature, but understandable in view of the daunting prospect of having to follow in the wake of such an illustrious incumbent as Carducci. In addition there was the inconvenient fact that the Chair was not one of Classics, but one of Romance literature. Pascoli knew that it was a mistake to leave Pisa and within a few months of his Bologna inaugural (9 January 1906) he was regretting the move. He was much disturbed by the knowledge that critics inside and outside the university were comparing him unfavourably with his predecessor. These critics became more vocal after Carducci's death in February 1907, driving the poet to occasional outbursts of irritation and despair. The reservations that were expressed about Pascoli's professional competence at Bologna seem to have been justified in the main considering the limited range of his lectures (Carducci had been exceptional for the breadth of his erudition), their somewhat tenuous intellectual content (to judge from *dispense* that have survived) and the unsystematic manner of their delivery (as reported by former pupils).

Amidst the multifarious duties connected with his university post Pascoli managed to produce a substantial amount of poetry. His most ambitious project was the long and complex work entitled *Le canzoni di re Enzio*, the historical materials for which were drawn from Italian thirteenth-century history. By the autumn of 1909 Pascoli had published the first three sections, which included the moving *Canzone dell'olifante*. In this third section (the first to be completed) the imprisoned king Enzio, immured in a tower in Bologna, listens to a troubadour's recitation of the death of Roland and recreates in his imagination the defeat and death of his own brother Manfred at the battle of Benevento in 1266, the event which inspired a famous passage in Dante's *Purgatorio* (Canto iii, lines 103–45). Two further sections and an epilogue had been planned for the work, but were never written. The poet did however complete the poems *Tolstoi* and *Rossini*, which joined *Paulo Ucello* (1903) in the volume *Poemi italici*, published in 1911. He also finished *Napoleone* and several more compositions destined for his *Poemi del Risorgimento*. He continued to compete for the Hoeufft prize with his Latin poetry and continued to win the gold medal: in 1909 with *Pomponia Graecina*, in 1910 with *Fanum Vacunae* and in 1911 with *Thallusa* (his thirteenth 'gold'). The poems with which he greeted the anniversary year 1911 — the hymn to Rome and the hymn to Turin — appeared in both a Latin and an Italian version.

The year 1911 was a climactic one in several ways. For Pascoli it was his last active year before succumbing to the stomach cancer which was already painful. It was also the fiftieth anniversary of the proclamation of the Kingdom of Italy (17 March 1861). At Bologna the poet opened his lecture course with the commemorative address *Nel Cinquantenario della patria*: in April he travelled to Livorno to address the cadets at the naval academy (*Italia!*). Finally in September came a dramatic event to crown this year of patriotic fervour: the launching of the military expedition to Tripolitania. 'L'Italia ha ripreso la sua via', wrote Pascoli to a friend. 'È impresa di civiltà contro la corruzione di decadenza, è impresa di liberazione.' Towards the end of November, two months after the outbreak of hostilities. Pascoli went to Barga at the request of the commune and delivered the last of his orations, *La grande proletaria s'è mossa*: a spirited celebration and justification of Italy's colonial war, which assorts ill with his earlier declarations about the brotherhood of man.

The decision to occupy Libya by force shows the extent and intensity of nationalist feeling in Italy at this moment, barely a year after the newly-formed Nationalist Party had held its first congress. The only organized opposition to the war came from the Socialist Party, a prominent member of which — Benito Mussolini — was sent to gaol in 1911 for organizing popular demonstrations against the campaign. But even the Socialists were not united on the issue, for some leading moderates had been won over by the argument that it was in the vital interests of the country to provide an outlet for Italy's unemployed. This was one of the arguments deployed by Pascoli in his Barga address, and it links up with his longstanding concern for the plight of the Italian emigrant worker expressed in the poem *Italy* and elsewhere. The other key to understanding his enthusiasm for the war is to be found in the view of patriotism which he was promulgating in this year of national celebration. For Pascoli patriotism is the cement that binds the social classes together; it is the animating force which transcends all sectional interests; it is what is needed to transform the ethnic and cultural entity 'Italy' into a sociopolitical entity, Italy the nation-state. For him therefore a successful colonial war was proof not only that the Italian nation had become a political reality, but also that the Italian working-class — conspicuously absent from the struggle for unity during the Risorgimento — had now, by virtue of donning uniform and fighting under the Italian flag, become integrated with the rest of the nation. This view would have had greater validity if it could have been shown that the proletarian members of the rank and file of the expeditionary force had spontaneously chosen their role as colonizers. But characteristically Pascoli speaks from his heart and not with his head. Carried away by his vision of the 'third' Italy taking up again the civilizing mission of classical Rome (the 'first' Italy), he closed his mind to the obvious objections to the Libyan enterprise: its injustice towards the indigenous population of Tripolitania and its impracticality, on account of the barren nature of the terrain, as a way of providing living space and an immediate livelihood for unemployed Italian labourers. As it turned out, the expected mass exodus of agricultural workers from Italy never took place, and the dream of an African desert blooming again under their ministrations was not realized. However, the success or failure of the campaign was less important in Pascoli's eyes than the event itself. The proletarian nation ('la grande proletaria') had descended to the field of battle and proved her strength: 'Così l'Italia si è affermata e confermata.' Such is the gist of Pascoli's peroration and the meaning of the title of his address.

The Barga oration was Pascoli's last public engagement before he died. His doctors already knew that his stomach pains were due to a malignant growth which was inoperable. In February 1912 he travelled back to his house in Bologna, where he died on Easter Saturday (6 April) with Maria at his bedside.

Another celebrated writer of Pascoli's generation who had recently died was the poet and novelist Antonio Fogazzaro (1842—1911), and the two deaths occurring so close together seemed to mark the passing away of the nineteenth century in Italian letters. D'Annunzio was still at work on the *Laudi*: the fourth book, *Merope*, celebrating the war in Libya, was published in 1912, and his *Contemplazione della morte* (inspired in part by Pascoli's death) came out in the same year. But d'Annunzio, too, was approaching the end of his poetic career, for although his début as a man of action in the war years was still a little way off, *Merope* virtually exhausted his lyrical vein. Already new voices had made themselves heard and were speaking with unmistakably twentieth-century accents. Pirandello, by now established as a novelist and short-story writer, was beginning his career as a dramatist, and the new poets had turned away from d'Annunzio's lyrical abandon to cultivate a more secret Muse. Gozzano's *Colloqui* and Saba's *Poesie* appeared in 1911. Campana's *Canti Orfici* (1914) would be published within two years of Pascoli's death, and Rebora, Sbarbaro and Jahier were all at work.

II

Within days of Pascoli's death, a tribute from Gabriele d'Annunzio appeared in the Rome newspaper *Giornale d'Italia*, which made a startling pronouncement concerning the stature and originality of the dead poet: 'Giovanni Pascoli è il piú grande e originale poeta apparso in Italia dopo il Petrarca. Questo sarà riconosciuto quando l'Itália rinnoverà anche le vecchie tavole dei valori poetici.' There is more than a little pious exaggeration in these words of praise, and it is inconceivable that Pascoli could ever come to be regarded as the peer of Petrarch, out-ranking even Leopardi. Nevertheless, some part at least of d'Annunzio's prediction was fulfilled, for when two more generations of poets had come and gone, and the poetic movements of the first half of the twentieth century came to be charted, Pascoli's position alongside d'Annunzio as a forerunner of the modern lyric was clear to see. To Luciano Anceschi compiling his anthology *Lirica del Novecento* in 1953 the choice of a starting-point lay between the *Crepuscolari* on the one hand, Pascoli and d'Annunzio on the other; and although in the event he chose the former option, for reasons that are explained in his preface and elsewhere,[3] he recognized that with somewhat different criteria it would have been equally logical to commence the anthology with '*certo* Pascoli ... *certo* d'Annunzio'.[4] Alfredo Schiaffini, writing in the wake of Anceschi's anthology, put the case for Pascoli's 'modernity' in even more outspoken terms: 'Il momento cruciale, il salto del fosso, nella storia del nostro linguaggio poetico, sono rappresentati dalla poesia di Giovanni Pascoli.'[5] Schiaffini's article — 'Giovanni Pascoli disintegratore della forma poetica tradizionale' — was one of many substantial contributions made to Pascoli scholarship during the period of the centenary celebration honouring the hundredth anniversary of the poet's birth. Like other contributions in the same vein, it confirmed and developed the views expressed in 1936 by Walter Binni,[6] who, together with Domenico Petrini,[7] was one of the first critics to situate Pascoli in the framework of *Decadentismo*, relating his poetic technique to the theory and practice of other — chiefly French — innovators of the late nineteenth century. Schiaffini and Contini[8] initiated the detailed linguistic studies of Pascoli which still constitute a fruitful line of investigation. At the same time the poet's 'decadence' has been the subject of psychological, political and ideological analyses; but the studies along these lines by Carlo Salinari,[9] Claudio Varese[10] and others, valuable as they are in helping to define Pascoli's place in the culture of the *fin de siècle*, do not illuminate the area which is of immediate concern here, namely the nature of the language and techniques that make up Pascoli's individual poetic style.

In their own way and within the limits imposed by a conservative temperament, Pascoli's innovations were as significant for the history of Italian poetry as were those of the *Symbolistes* for the development of the lyric in France. This having been said, it should not be thought, however, that the Italian poet intended to start a new movement or that he elaborated, like some of his French contemporaries, radically new theories about poetic language and technique. Echoes of pronouncements on the subject by Mallarmé and Claudel may be found in the writings of d'Annunzio, but not in those of Pascoli. Moreover, in view of the very different poetic traditions and personalities involved, it would be surprising if one were to find in the works of the Italian poet the specific influence of Mallarmé, Verlaine or any of the other poets at work in France whilst Pascoli's style was maturing. Attempts to trace these influences have all been inconclusive,[11] except in the case of the *Poemi conviviali*, which seem to owe something to Parnassian influence. At the same time, one cannot rule out the possibility that Pascoli's poetic methods may have been affected in a general way by an awareness of what his French contemporaries were doing. The more obvious affinities between him and them are: a new feeling for the sensuous and symbolic value of words, as distinct from their logical connotations; a tendency to reject explicit statement in favour of suggestion and implication; the development of a technique of versification aimed at avoiding sonority; the use of a more relaxed diction that is expressive without being elevated, solemn or oratorical.

Pascoli's technical expertise was evident from the outset. D'Annunzio drew attention to it in his review of the 1892 edition of *Myricae* and was to repeat his admiring comments two decades later, after the poet's death: 'Penso che nessun artefice moderno abbia posseduto l'arte sua come Giovanni Pascoli la possedeva ... Nessuno meglio di lui sapeva e dimostrava come l'arte non sia se non una magia pratica' (*Contemplazione della morte*). This fulsome tribute gains in significance from the fact that in one area of the poet's craft — the choice and handling of metre — the paths followed by the two poets had diverged, d'Annunzio taking up *vers libre* in pursuit of greater freedom and musicality, whilst Pascoli preferred to demonstrate his craftsman's delight in technical problems by staying with and exploring the limitations of closed metrical schemes, avoiding monotony by the use of a wide variety of metres and stanza-forms. A striking example of his originality in this field was his frequent use of the *novenario*, a metre almost wholly ignored by poets in the literary as distinct from the folk tradition, except for the sporadic use of it by some earlier nineteenth-century poets. Carducci had made it a constituent of some of his neoclassical metres, but used it only once — in *Jaufré Rudel* — as an Italian metre in its own right. Clearly it was not a metre that recommended itself to Italian poets, perhaps because, unlike the *endecasillabo*, it can generate only three distinctly different rhythmic patterns: iambic (based on the rhythmic unit ◡,), trochaic-dactylic (based on the rhythmic units of the trochee ,◡ and dactyl ,◡◡) and dactylo-anapaestic (based on the dactyl ,◡◡ and anapaest ◡◡,). In addition, the *novenario* tends to be monotonously regular: it shares with shorter lines the limitation that it is not long enough to accommodate a switch in mid-line from ascending to descending rhythm, or vice versa; at the same time the two extra syllables compared with the *settenario* merely add the extra rhythmic unit which causes monotony.

In practice the commonest form of the *novenario*, and the one most often used by Pascoli, has a dactylo-anapaestic movement:

la víta fu vána parvénza (*Allora*, 11)

The trochaic-dactylic form is very rarely found before Pascoli — and not at all in the literary tradition, according to Emilio Bigi[12] — but Pascoli uses it not infrequently, and it is exemplified by three poems in this selection:

Tútto pénde tácito e tétro (*La servetta di monte*, 8)

The iambic variety, also rare and the form least used by Pascoli, is the one with the most regular movement:

María restáva al fócoláre (*Il compagno dei taglialegna*, 21)

Considering that the *novenario* was unfamiliar to the contemporary reader and that its insistent rhythm must have sounded in more sensitive ears as a cacophony, Pascoli's adoption of it and his use of it in some cases in an unattenuated form, without any attempt to disguise its monotony, was audacious. Of course, given the right emotional content or subject-matter, the strong character of the metre in one or other of its forms may serve an expressive purpose; such is the case with the racing rhythms of the dactylo-anapaestic *novenario* employed in *La canzone del girarrosto*, which is all bustle from start to finish. But similar considerations do not apply to, say, *La Siréna*, which is written in the same metre. In this poem, and in a number of others in the selection, the metre, so far from being subservient to the content, is an intrusive element, and it must be said that on the whole Pascoli achieves a happier result either by combining the *novenario* with some other metre as a way of reining back its impetuous movement (the technique adopted in *La poesia*, *Nebbia* and *Il sonnellino*), or by combining two different forms of the *novenario*. This second method is successfully used as a structural device in *Il gelsomino notturno*, where a separate and distinct form of the *novenario* is used for each of the two narrative sequences: dactylo-anapaestic for the description of events in the house, trochaic-dactylic for the description of events in the garden. A different but equally artful use of structural rhythm is made in *La voce*, in which two types of *novenario* alternate with each other from line to line:

> C'è una voce nella mia vita,
> che avverto nel punto che muore;
> voce stanca, voce smarrita,
> col tremito del batticuore: (*La voce*, 1–4)

The overall effect is of a regular surging movement to and fro, the insistent pulses of energy of the trochaic line seeming to dissipate themselves in the anapaestic movement of the line that follows. The precise nature of the reader's response to this subliminal emotional stimulus will vary with the individual (Pascoli himself regarded the trochaic line as having a *molle cadenza*[13]), but clearly the combined rhythmic movement is a musical device designed to underscore the complex of contrasting emotions expressed in the poem: anguish and resignation, despair and reassurance. As such, it operates in conjunction with the other obvious musical device in the poem — the refrain — to sustain a high level of emotional intensity.

The examples so far quoted are all, with the single exception of the fourth line of *La voce*, lines in which there is complete coincidence of speech-accent with metrical stress (ictus). But the art of versification might be said to be concerned less with the coincidence of accent and ictus than with their *non*-coincidence, the aim of the poet being to create a satisfying tension between the metrical pattern and spontaneous speech-rhythms in the manner explained by Pascoli in his letter to Giuseppe Chiarini on the subject of neoclassical metres.[14] This was an area in which he broke new ground, going further than any of his predecessors in loosening the bonds of metre to the point at which, as later examples will illustrate, the line as a metrical unit seems to break down completely.

Three basic devices are available to the poet for creating his rhythmic counterpoint, the first of which (the displacement of speech-accents with respect to metrical stresses) is illustrated by the fourth line of *La voce: col tremito del batticuore*. The metrical 'hiccough' in this line is caused by the fact that in syllables five and six the natural voice-accents (unaccented *del*, followed by a secondary stress on the first syllable of *batticuore*) reverse the order required by the metre (′ ⌣); consequently it is necessary, in reading the line, to promote slightly the syllable *del* to enable it to support the ictus, and to reduce the natural voice-stress on the following syllable so that it becomes virtually atonic: *batticuòre*.

The rest of *La voce* offers good examples, not only of the displacement phenomenon already illustrated, but also of the other devices used to conceal the regularity of the metrical structure: enjambement (which blurs or obliterates the division between consecutive lines) and the positioning of syntactical pauses at places other than line-endings in such a manner as to disturb or arrest the rhythmic flow. These devices are displayed to particularly good advantage in the third and fourth sections of the poem (lines 25—48). Syntactical breaks are occasioned by the use of parentheses such as (*ancora!*), (*nel carcere!*), the exclamatory nature of which adds to their force as line-stoppers, and the movement is also arrested by the introduction of direct speech: *dissi — 'Avresti . . . ora, o babbo!' —* (lines 39—41). In the long period beginning *Una notte . . .* (line 37) and ending eleven lines later, the syntactical divisions cut right across the line-divisions, and even across stanza-divisions at one point (lines 40—1). Pascoli's handling of metre in these same two sections of the poem has other points of interest. Line 33 is a hypermetric line, which has been irregularly lengthened in order to draw out the pathos: *Non far piangere piangere piangere* (a *decasillabo sdrucciolo*). It has eleven syllables, the last of which must be read as part of the line following, so as to produce the requisite rhyme with line 35: *piange-, ange-*. But this still leaves line 33 with ten syllables instead of nine. Line 36, on the other hand, is a syllable short and requires the last syllable of *angelo* to make up the proper number. Pascoli uses hypermetric rhymes to particularly good effect in *La canzone del girarrosto* to speed up the tempo, and in general his use of them is sufficiently frequent for them to count almost as a hallmark of his style. Although he is bolder than earlier poets, he is rarely as audacious as in the example of the line *non far piangere . . .*, and the normal situation is that the extra syllable or syllables of a hypermetric line are absorbed by the line following, as for example in *La voce*, 77f. One other modification of metre for expressive effect is to be noted in this poem at line 40, which departs from the anticipated dactylo-anapaestic pattern, repeating instead the trochaic rhythm of line 39. The mild shock of surprise thus caused serves as a form of emphasis.

Although Pascoli's use of the *novenario* was an interesting innovation in itself, it was less significant from the point of view of subsequent developments in the history of the Italian lyric than his handling of the most traditional and most expressive of all the Italian metres, the *endecasillabo*. Here the full extent of his innovatory technique was more readily apparent to contemporary readers, for there was a centuries-old tradition with which to make comparisons, going back through Foscolo and Leopardi to Dante and Petrarch. The techniques of versification he used were similar to the ones employed in the *novenario*, but the more complex structure of the longer line made it more amenable to manipulation, and in its extreme form his method of versification succeeded in attenuating the potential sonority of the *endecasillabo* to the level of a conversational whisper. Before illustrating this, it is necessary, however, to make a few preliminary observations of an elementary kind about the structure of the hendecasyllabic line.

Unlike the *novenario*, which has only one predetermined metrical stress coincident with voice-accent (namely, the stress on the eighth syllable), the *endecasillabo* has two, one of which falls immutably on the tenth syllable of every line, whilst the other is variable and need not occupy the same position in any two consecutive lines. In the poetry of the central tradition from Dante down to Carducci this 'moveable main stress' — which, like the ictus on the tenth syllable, must coincide with a voice-accent — usually falls on the fourth or sixth syllable and produces a climactic or turning point near the middle of the line, dividing it into two unequal halves, each with a distinctive rhythm conferred on it by the disposition of secondary accents. The two halves of the *endecasillabo*, each of which is a line of verse regularly constituted, may have the same or different rhythmic movements, so that much more variety is possible than in any of the shorter metres. It is quite regular, though naturally less common, for the moveable main stress to come before the fourth syllable, and in conjunction with a strong stress later in the line it may give rise to a tripartite division. In this case the line is said to have two 'caesuras', the term being here used to denote the break between words occurring at the point where the hendecasyllabic line divides into its constituent parts. A third caesura is not normally tolerated in the mainline tradition, because it threatens the unity of the line; therefore, if the poet does use one, it is deliberately in order to create an impression of fragmentation and unrhythmic movement.

It is now possible to illustrate the novelty of Pascoli's method of versification in the hendecasyllabic line, a novelty which shows itself in the manner in which syntax is fitted (or rather, *not* fitted) to the metrical divisions of the line. The traditional method, widely used by Pascoli at all stages of his poetic career, was to accommodate syntactical pauses to the metrical divisions, thus producing an impression of solidity, compactness and 'inevitability':

> Io prendo un po' di silice e di quarzo:
> lo fondo; aspiro; e soffio poi di lena:
> ve' la fïala, come un dí di marzo,
> azzurra e grigia, torbida e serena!   (*Contrasto*, 1–4)

A reader whose ear has become attuned to a robust melodic line of this sort is bound to be disorientated by the opening of a poem such as *Digitale purpurea* and wonder what kind of hendecasyllabic line it is, or whether it is a true *endecasillabo* at all:

> Siedono. L'una guarda l'altra. L'una
> esile e bionda . . .

Apart from having eleven syllables with a regular ictus on the tenth, the first line exhibits none of the conventional features of the traditional *endecasillabo*. The tonic accents are equally stressed, except possibly for a somewhat lighter stress on the tonic accent of *guarda*; consequently the line has no focal point and no metrical caesura. The syntax, however, breaks the line into three portions, of which the central one, a trochaic *senario*, is the only one regularly constituted from a metrical standpoint. The break after the ninth syllable occurs so late in the line that the words *L'una* seem to detach themselves and join the associated adjectives at the beginning of the next line. In short, the syntactical breaks almost completely mask the metrical structure of the line, which is a trochaic–dactylic *endecasillabo* without caesura: ′∪∪′∪′∪′∪′∪ It is instructive to compare this with a famous line by Petrarch, which shows exactly the same disposition of accents, but also has a caesura after the sixth syllable, producing a change of rhythm from descending to ascending, from trochaic–dactylic to iambic:

′ ∪ ∪ ′ ∪ ′|∪ ′ ∪ ′ ∪
Movesi il vecchierel canuto e bianco.

This single analysis must suffice as a pointer to the way in which Pascoli often increases the tension between metre and natural speech-rhythm to the point at which the former begins to break down, allowing the latter to predominate. His characteristic technique, which occurs sporadically in early poems for specific purposes — in *Arano*, for example — is put to more general use from *Myricae* (1891) onwards, and is the norm in the *Poemetti* and *Poemi conviviali*.

Pascoli used many other metres apart from the two already discussed, and they are widely illustrated by the poems in this selection, but the only other feature of his metrics calling for comment here is his use of neoclassical measures exemplified by the Sapphic stanzas incorporated into *Solon*. Numerous attempts have been made in many different languages over the centuries to recreate classical measures, and more than one scheme has been devised for adapting the accentual systems of modern European languages to the quantitative metres of Latin poetry. Generally speaking, the more successful methods, such as Carducci's in Italian, have recognized the artificiality of treating the syllables of a modern language as having, either intrinsically or by position, a quantitative aspect. Carducci made no attempt to imitate classical scansion, but instead combined regularly constituted Italian metres in such a way as to construct lines with the correct number of syllables and with rhythms similar to those of classical poetry read not quantitatively, but accentually. The simplest method of adaptation, however, is to substitute accentual feet for quantitative feet, treating accented and unaccented syllables as the equivalents of long and short syllables respectively. Familiar examples abound in English, as for example Coleridge's elegiac couplet:

In the hexameter rises the fountain's silvery column;
  In the pentameter aye falling in melody back.

This may be compared with Tennyson's attempt at the same metre using a quantitative method:

Hexameters no worse than daring Germany gave us,
  Barbarous experiment, barbarous hexameters.

Pascoli's method is nearer to Coleridge's than to Tennyson's, but he had at his disposal one resource not available to English poets, namely the quality of Italian vowel-sounds, which permits any tonic syllable to be prolonged without wholly destroying the character of the word. In recognition of this, the first rule of Pascoli's *Regole di metrica neoclassica*[15] states that: 'I versi neoclassici devono essere pronunziati con intensità d'accenti, scolpendo e prolungando le sillabe legittimamente accentate.' Later rules specify the circumstances in which atonic syllables, too, are *allungabili*. By putting these principles into practice, he achieves a closer correspondence than Coleridge did between accent-based metres and the quantitative scansion of classical poetry.

It is only a short step from neoclassical stanzas to stanza-forms in general, the last topic for discussion under the heading of prosody and metrics. Many of Pascoli's poems were written in long-established forms belonging to the Italian literary tradition: the sonnet and madrigal for short compositions, *endecasillabi sciolti* for long ones. *Terza rima*, traditionally the metre of long poems like the epic or the *capitolo*, is used by Pascoli for short lyrics too. In addition, the waning folk tradition furnished him with other ready-made stanza-forms, his use of the ballad and *strambotto*[16] being more than just a metrical exercise (as it had been for Carducci) and yet not motivated, as with the early Romantics, by an interest in popular poetry for its own sake. His comparative indifference towards the purity of the genre shows itself in the readiness with which he adapted popular forms (as in *Nevicata*), or created hybrid ones out of a contamination of the popular with the literary tradition (*Lo stornello, Lavandare*). Such procedures may indeed be *alessandrinismo*,[17] but they in no way invalidate Pascoli's method of exploiting the short *schemata* of the popular tradition: even where his adaptations are less than faithful to the spirit of the originals, they are not on that account any the less aesthetically consonant with the style and content of other poems of *Myricae* with a rural setting. It is curious that Pascoli never employed the noblest of all Italian lyric metres in the literary tradition, the *canzone*. Perhaps its complex structure would have been too tight a strait-jacket for his purposes, though many of the stanza-forms that he devised for *Canti di Castelvecchio* are extremely intricate. An idea of their complexity can be got from the metrical notes accompanying individual poems in this selection, and no further comment is called for here, except to draw attention to Pascoli's frequent and skilful use of the refrain as a structural or tonal device.

Speculation about the particular source or sources from which Pascoli may have derived his use of refrains does not seem very profitable. It has been strenuously maintained — and equally strongly denied — that he owed it to the theory and practice of Edgar Allan Poe: a plausible enough suggestion considering that Pascoli was acquainted with Poe's works and translated into Italian part of *The Raven*. On the other hand the device was not the sole prerogative of the American poet, and other near-contemporary models present themselves with equal plausibility, Tennyson being just one. The primary function of the refrain is to mark the divisions of the poem, and in doing this it can (as in *Il sonno di Odisseo*) undergo modifications that indicate a temporal or other progression. It may simultaneously serve as a tonal device for sustaining a particular mood or atmosphere, as is the case with onomatopoeic refrains like the *uuh . . . uuuh . . . uuuh* of *Notte di vento* (*Myricae*) and the *trr trr trr terit tirit* of *L'uccellino del freddo* (*Canti di Castelvecchio*). *La voce* is another poem with a refrain (*Zvani*) which performs both functions.

Turning now from metrics to the subject of poetic diction, the first feature deserving of comment is the colloquial syntax which Pascoli deploys over a wide area of his poetic production and which has been regarded as possibly the most noteworthy innovation introduced by him into Italian poetry.[18] Its characteristics have already been seen in connection with the method of versification used in *La voce*, which is a good illustration of the use of the parentheses, interjections, suspensions and elliptical constructions typical of the disorganized medium of colloquial speech. The difference between this and the language of Pascoli's poetry is that the fragmentary utterances of the latter, even though they are not syntactically articulated, are nonetheless carefully orchestrated. There are two ways of looking at the peculiarities of Pascoli's poetic syntax. On the one hand, its fragmentation may be seen as a stylistic device intended to lower the level of the poetic discourse and so prevent the tone from becoming solemn and hieratical. It may also be the case, as Schiaffini has argued, that the absence of careful syntactical organization is symptomatic of a particular mode of vision and reflects an habitual way of seeing things as an assemblage of discrete particulars rather than as a synthetic whole. Pascoli's discursive prose proceeds in a comparable manner, the argument being developed by a succession of paratactic statements, between which it is sometimes difficult to make a logical connection.

Not surprisingly, in view of the fact that much of his poetry aims at an effect of almost prosaic matter-of-factness, Pascoli was sparing in his use of literary images. To English readers, familiar with the richly figurative language of much English poetry, his diction must appear wanting in this respect, though it is less chaste and 'classical' than, say, Leopardi's. Pascoli's literary images, though relatively scarce, can be striking and highly expressive, as the following examples show. In the first illustration (*La siepe*, 1–3) the image serves to reinforce a sentiment (possessiveness):

> Siepe del mio campetto, utile e pia,
> che al campo sei *come l'anello al dito,*
> *che dice mia la donna che fu mia.*

A more complex example is the following, which occurs in *Il lampo*, 4–7.

> bianca bianca nel tacito tumulto
> una casa apparí sparí d'un tratto;
> *come un occhio, che, largo, esterrefatto*
> *s'aprí si chiuse*, nella notte nera.

The simile is a graphic one, but its expressiveness is not confined to the visual dimension, and the emotional component is equally important. The image of terror brings to a climax the series of metaphors used earlier in the poem to suggest a landscape convulsed with fear (*terra ansante . . . in sussulto*) under a storm-racked sky (*cielo . . . tragico, disfatto*). The description is not really conceived in naturalistic terms at all, but calls to mind the expressionistic landscapes of Van Gogh, where the distorted and contorted outlines are manifestations of the painter's own feelings of uneasiness. Another noteworthy use of imagery is the *Albeggia Dio*! of *La pecorella smarrita*, line 11. Here the image, which clothes with sensuous form an abstract idea (the second coming of Christ) is rooted in the metaphorical language of Christian mysticism, and would not have been unworthy of Dante. Finally, one should call attention to Pascoli's use of synaesthetic images, some of which are particularly memorable, like the *pigolío di stelle* in *Il gelsomino notturno* (line 16) or the *cader fragile* (*di foglie*) in *Novembre* (line 11).

A second reason for the comparative infrequency of images in Pascoli's poetry is to be found in the nature of his descriptive technique. Depiction of the exterior aspects of reality features prominently in his work, and his chief concern here is with achieving the maximum of immediacy and precision. For this purpose he relies, broadly speaking, on a strictly proper, non-figurative use of words. He supplements the generic vocabulary of traditional Italian poetry with dialectalisms and with specialized vocabularies appropriate to a rather more technical register, notably in the fields of botany and ornithology. His method is selective and focusses sharply on individual details: 'il passero saputo in cor già gode, / e il tutto spia dai rami irti del moro' (*Arano*, 7f); the robin 'fa un salto, un frullo, un giro, un volo; / molleggia, piú qui, piú lí' (*Il compagno dei taglialegna*, 15f). In the descriptive context metaphors tend to be chosen for their aptness and capacity for graphic representation: the mistletoe berry is a 'pearl' (*Il vischio*, 65); the flowers of the Persian acacia are 'pink plumes' (*Romagna*, 28). English readers may be reminded of the descriptive manner of Tennyson (e.g. 'more crumpled than a poppy from the sheath'), another poet with an eye for the characteristic detail in nature. The proliferation of plant- and bird-names in Pascoli's poetry, so different from the conservatism and sobriety of Leopardi's vocabulary, is regarded by many as a fault, but a comparison of Pascoli's 'landscapes' with those of Leopardi's idylls reveals how different they are in conception and how wrong it is to judge the success of one in terms of the techniques used in the other. A generic vocabulary was entirely appropriate for Leopardi's purpose, for his idylls were concerned with the universal, not with the particular in nature, and the scenes he painted were not ends in themselves, but metaphors of the human condition or correlatives of his own thoughts, feelings and emotions. In contrast to this procedure, Pascoli's 'poetica degli oggetti' requires a vocabulary that can differentiate between blackbirds and bullfinches, myrtles and mulberries, saucepans and stewpots. This entails the use of a precise nomenclature as a way of evoking accurately and succinctly, without circumlocution, the object denoted. The theoretical justification for this is given in a previously mentioned passage of *Il fanciullino* (Section XIV, pp. 43f), where Pascoli complains of the generic nature of the Italian literary language and of the difficulty of finding, in Italian, words to denote common objects:

> Il nome loro non è fatto, o non è divulgato, o non è comune a tutta la nazione o a tutte le classi del popolo. Pensate ai fiori e agli uccelli ... S'ha sempre a dire uccelli, sí di quelli che fanno *tottaví* e sí di quelli che fanno *crocro*? Basta dir fiori o fioretti, e aggiungere, magari, vermigli e gialli, e non far distinzione tra un greppo coperto di margherite e un prato gremito di crochi?

The poetic vocabulary envisaged by Pascoli is in danger of failing in its purpose as a means of communication through being unintelligible, and there is a limit beyond which even a sympathetic reader is not prepared to keep reaching for the dictionary. D'Annunzio quite often ignored this limit and became precious, indulging his interest in rare words for their own sake. Pascoli, on the other hand, kept his philological enthusiasm under tighter control,[19] recognizing perhaps that readers cannot be expected to follow the poet too far into the semantic stratosphere, and mindful also that the use of unfamiliar terminology, if it is to be acceptable, must remain a means to an end, not become an end in itself. Similar considerations apply to his use of dialect words, which means to a small extent the dialect of Romagna, but principally those of the Tuscan Maremma and the Garfagnana. These words are justified by their expressive function in providing local colour, but the author knew that a regional vocabulary would be incomprehensible to the wider reading public; he therefore added a glossary to the second edition of *Canti di Castelvecchio*.

Another problem raised by Pascoli's poetic vocabulary concerns his over-frequent use of elementary onomatopoeic effects like the ones in the following quotation from *The Hammerless Gun* in *Canti di Castelvecchio*:

> E me segue un *tac tac* di capinere,
> e me segue un *tin tin* di pettirossi,
> un *zisteretetet* di cincie, un *rererere*
> di cardellini.

These onomatopoeic expressions, unlike dialectalisms and technical words, cannot be criticized for incomprehensibility, nor is there any question but that they fulfil their expressive function admirably at the sensory level, but most readers and critics reject them as being too crude or too infantile. It is possible to rationalize the objection in artistic terms by saying that the use of pure onomatopoeia disrupts the linguistic medium of intelligible words, substituting pure sound for the semantic dimension. Consequently they are an intrusive element in the poem analogous in their effect to the sound of real cannon in the *1812 Overture*. On these grounds poems relying heavily on elementary onomatopoeia have been excluded from the selection, with the result that a well-known feature of Pascolian diction is sparsely represented in it.

After what has just been said about the exactness and 'particularity' of Pascoli's descriptive technique, it must seem paradoxical that the last section of this introduction begins by illustrating the procedures of suggestion and concealment, which work in a diametrically opposite direction. Such, however, is the case with many of Pascoli's most successful and original lyrics. They combine clarity and precision in individual details with a certain vagueness of the overall picture, sometimes with uncertainty about the exact implications of the poem. Indeed, it is in the nature of any poetry which, unlike 'classically' conceived compositions, works through implication and allusion instead of through explicit statement, that it leaves room for individual interpretation. One of the reasons for its appeal is that it acts as a stimulus for imaginings that may never succeed in finding a definite resting-place. It should be stated, however, that unlike some examples of French *Symbolisme*, Pascoli's lyrics, even when their meaning is ambiguous, do not lend themselves to completely open-ended interpretations. Moreover, it is by no means the general rule that his poems imply second meanings over and above their overt signification; in fact the opposite is the norm in his earlier poems. *Arano*, for example, is typical of the kind of poem which works exclusively at the descriptive level. But a comparison of *Arano* with *Lavandare* shows how slight an addition is needed to change a descriptive scene into something quite different. Neither the title of the latter poem, nor the descriptive details of the first six lines (a plough standing unattended in a field; the sound of women singing; the splash and thud of clothes being washed in the water of the mill-stream) prepare the reader for the emotive ending in which are heard the words of the *strambotto* that the washerwomen are singing in the distance:

> Il vento soffia e nevica la frasca,
> e tu non torni ancora al tuo paese!
> quando partisti, come son rimasta!
> come l'aratro in mezzo alla maggese.

The words of the song operate retrospectively on the opening lines of the poem, changing them from landscape description into a metaphor of the deserted woman's sense of loss. A similar transformation is brought about in *Carrettiere* by the interjection of a single question: 'che mai diceva il querulo aquilone / che muggía nelle forre e fra le grotte?' A simple description of country life is thus turned into a poem about the contrast between the blissful existence of dreams and the harshness of waking reality.

The procedures used in *Lavandare* and *Carrettiere* (both

published in the *Myricae* of 1894) recur in later poems such as *L'ora di Barga* (1900), in which the reader is made to realize at the end of the poem (but only then) that the message of the striking clock is more than just a reminder that the evening is advancing and that it is time to go indoors. During the intervening period Pascoli had begun — rather in the manner of Leopardi in *La ginestra* — to use an overtly symbolic metaphor as the starting-point and central organizing principle of a poem. The method is used in *Il nunzio* (one of the later *Myricae*) and in a number of the *Poemetti* and the *Canti di Castelvecchio*, including several in this selection: *Il libro, Digitale purpurea, La quercia caduta* and *La poesia*. In all these examples the purport of the symbolic image is defined by the context in which it is used. Not so, however, recurring images like the cypress-tree, the nest, the isolated house or the sound of bells, to which precise meanings are less easily attached. Such images are superficially indistinguishable from the purely descriptive elements that accompany them, but the fact that they occur repeatedly and are highly charged with emotion gives them a privileged status beyond that of 'properties' in a naturalistic description. They are private symbols, which relate not only to the poet's environment, but also and more significantly to his inner world of anxieties, preoccupations and fears. To be more explicit, they connect up with Pascoli's feelings of insecurity, his preoccupation with death and his timidity with respect to personal relationships outside the family circle.

The poem *Il gelsomino notturno*, written to celebrate a friend's marriage, is a unique example of the technique of allusiveness. As pointed out in the notes, the poem follows faithfully the tradition of the classical epithalamium in expressing the hope that the marriage will be blessed with children, but there is no open reference to the love-making of the wedding-night, only a description of lights going out in the house as the couple retires to bed, and an allusion to the fertilization of the flower in the garden.

Equally original, considering the date at which they were written and the bold way in which they break with traditional methods of poetic organization, are poems like *Patria, La tessitrice* and others not in our selection, which use the device sometimes called *l'inizio a indovinello*. The true subject of the poem, or the precise nature of the situation described, is concealed from the reader at the beginning and is made clear only at the end of the poem, where it may either come as a complete surprise or as the final stage of a progressive revelation.

It would be impossible to conclude this review of Pascoli's technical innovations without considering briefly his use of assonance and alliteration, although here the innovation lies not in the devices as such, but in the extent to which Pascoli uses them, either to enhance the melodic effect, or for a more specific purpose, mimetic, tonal or structural.[20] Of the poems in the selection, the ones most elaborately constructed as regards the sound-stratum are *Alba festiva*, which uses assonance for imitative and tonal purposes, and *L'ora di Barga*, which combines assonance with word-repetition and rhythmic effects to produce an atmosphere of torpor. Precisely because of the extent to which these poems rely for effect on the manipulation of sound, they seem a little too contrived for modern tastes, and may be rejected by some readers on that account. *Alba festiva*, for instance, is constructed on the basis of no fewer than three series of assonances. There is a long sequence associated with the sound of the bell with the voice of gold (*ronzano* − or − oro − *implori* − *sonoro* − *Adoro*), another long one associated with the bell with the voice of silver (*squillano* − *tintinno* − *squilla* − *argentina* − *Dilla, dilla* − *tranquilla*), and finally a shorter one associated with the idea of the tomb (*profonda* − *rimbomba* − *risponda* − *tomba*). The effect is anything but subtle, and would hardly warrant further comment were it not for the fact that certain misconceptions about the operation of sound in poetry take a long time to die. It is therefore necessary to stress that, with the exception of genuinely onomatopoeic words like 'crash', 'bang', 'plop', the sound of words is only a *potential* source of expressive effect, and requires the assistance of meaning or context in order to become actually expressive in a specific manner. Thus in *Alba festiva* the meanings of certain key words have a crucial part to play in actualizing the potential for expressiveness latent in the contrasting vowel-sounds *o* and *i*. If we ascribe a full, resonant sound to the vowel *o* in the first series of assonances, it is because of the meaning of the word *ronzano* and the notions of opulence associated with gold. Likewise the thinner sound ascribed to *i* depends partly on the meaning of *squillano* (often used of shrill sounds), partly on the onomatopoeic *tintinno*, and partly on the less opulent associations of the word for silver. Finally, the effect produced by the third sequence, which is no longer imitative but tonal, depends in part on the onomatopoeic *rimbomba*, in part on the meanings of the words *profonda* and *tomba*. Assonance and alliteration are not always used by Pascoli in such an obvious manner, and their effectiveness seems to increase the more discreetly they are employed. In *Novembre*, for instance, both devices are used to obtain sensorial effects, but they pass almost unnoticed at a first reading. Other poems in the selection (for example *Patria* and *Orfano*) use assonance and alliteration with equal success.

In conclusion, the reader should be reminded that this rapid survey of Pascoli's innovations was undertaken with the specific and limited aim of illustrating the features of his work which were important for the subsequent development of Italian poetry. The approach is not intended to imply that technical brilliance is synonymous with poetic excellence. In fact, some of Pascoli's worst failures were occasioned precisely by technical expertise carried to excess in ways that have been adequately discussed by Croce and other critics. Since this anthology aims to present some of the best of Pascoli, whilst excluding completely the worst, it is to be hoped that none of the poems in it can be cited as examples of misplaced ingenuity, but throughout the work of selection the doubt was always present that a foreigner may be more tolerant of speciousness than a native reader, less able that is to discriminate between the skill which produces the well-wrought masterpiece and the skill which, to a more refined ear, reveals itself as artifice and nothing more. Although this doubt persists, it is mitigated by d'Annunzio's unqualified expressions of admiration for Pascoli's technical ability. D'Annunzio found nothing to criticize in Pascoli's onomatopoeic effects, in his use of bird-names, or in most of the mannerisms which so exasperated Croce. Could it be that Pascoli is essentially a poet's poet?

NOTES

1 Page-references are to *Prose*, Milan, Mondadori, 1971, vol. i, as are also later references to the Messina *Discorsi*.

2 For critics who (like Petrini) interpret the *Fanciullino* as an apology for pure aestheticism, or who (like Barberi Squarotti) regard it as primarily a psychological document evidencing infantile regression, it is of course easy to relate the essay to every phase of Pascoli's poetic

output. See D. Petrini, *Dal Barocco al Decadentismo*, Florence, 1957, ii.181–301; G. Barberi Squarotti, *Simboli e strutture della poesia del Pascoli*, Messina, Florence, 1966. Cf. also M. Valgimigli (see Bibliography).

3 'Pascoli verso il Novecento', *Studi* (1962) iii.15–34 (see Bibliography: Centenary Miscellanies).

4 *Lirica del Novecento*, Florence, 1963[3], Introduction, xvi.

5 In the symposium *Omaggio a Giovanni Pascoli nel centenario della nascita*, Milan, 1955, 240.

6 *La poetica del decadentismo*.

7 *Op. cit.* above, in note 2. Petrini's Pascoli essays first appeared in *Civiltà Moderna* in 1929 and 1930.

8 See Bibliography.

9 *Miti e coscienza del decadentismo italiano*, Milan, 1960, 107–83.

10 'La poesia politica del P.' in *Pascoli politico, Tasso e altri saggi*, Milan, 1961, 241–54; *Pascoli decadente*, Florence, 1964, Pt.ii: 'Decadentismo e politica in *Odi e Inni*'.

11 For influences on the youthful Pascoli, see G. Petrocchi, *La formazione letteraria di Giovanni Pascoli*, Florence, 1953. For the mature poet, see: W. Binni, *La poetica del decadentismo*, Florence, 1969, 126; C. Pellegrini, 'Il P. e la Francia', *Omaggio* (cited in note 5), 317–20; M. Praz, 'G.P. e l'Inghilterra', *ibid.*, 321–7; F. Piemontese, 'Considerazioni sul ritmo nella poesia pascoliana', *ibid.*, 237–9; V. Lugli, 'Incontri di G.P. con la poesia francese', *Discorsi* (1958) 367–89 (see Bibliography: 'Centenary Miscellanies').

12 'La metrica delle poesie italiane del P.', *Studi* (1962) ii.29–56 (see Bibliography: Centenary Miscellanies).

13 'La poesia lirica in Roma', *Prose*, Milan, 1971, i.664.

14 *Prose*, i.939.

15 *Prose*, i.987–1007.

16 See introductory notes to poems No. 4, 12, 35 and 37.

17 V. Santoli, 'P. e la poesia popolare', *Studi* (1962) ii.75 (see Bibliography).

18 A. Jenni, 'P. tecnico', *Studi* (1962) ii.20 (see Bibliography).

19 For a different view cf. the studies of Petrini and Barberi Squarotti cited in note 2. The method of structural analysis, used by the latter critic without reference to complementary lines of approach, leads to unconvincing (though stimulating) conclusions.

20 The functioning of sound in Pascoli's poetry is fully investigated in Beccaria's *Metrica e sintassi nella poesia di G.P.*, ch. 3.

SELECT BIBLIOGRAPHY

Pascoli's works
Tutte le opere, Milan, Mondadori, 1939—52:
  I *Poesie*, 1939[1], 1971[12] (2 vols.) with a foreword by A. Baldini.
  II *Carmina*, 1951[1], 1970[5] (ed. M. Valgimigli).
  III *Prose* (2 vols.):
    vol. i *Pensieri di varia umanità*, 1946[1], 1971[4].
    vol. ii *Scritti danteschi*, 2 tomes (ed. A. Vicinelli) 1952[1], 1971[3].
The Italian poems are also available in Mondadori's 'Oscar' series: *Poesie* (3 vols.) 1968[1], 1974[3], with two essays by Gianfranco Contini: 'Profilo di Giovanni Pascoli', 'Il linguaggio di Pascoli'.

Biographies
Maria Pascoli, *Lungo la vita di Giovanni Pascoli* (Memorie curate e integrate da A. Vicinelli), Milan, Mondadori, 1961.
M. Biagini, *Il poeta solitario. Vita di Giovanni Pascoli*, 2nd edn., Milan, Mursia, 1963.

Centenary miscellanies
References given in the foot-notes are to the following:
Omaggio a Giovanni Pascoli nel centenario della nascita, Milan Mondadori, 1955.
Pascoli. Discorsi nel centenario della nascita, Bologna, Zanichelli, 1958.
Studi per il centenario della nascita di Giovanni Pascoli (Convegno bolognese, 28—30 marzo 1958) 3 vols., Bologna, Commissione per i testi di lingua, 1962.

CRITICAL STUDIES

In addition to the studies cited in notes to the Introduction, the following titles, arranged in chronological order, are recommended for further reading. For fuller bibliographical information consult: A. Prete, *La critica e Pascoli*, Bologna, Cappelli, 1975.

B. Croce, *Giovanni Pascoli: studio critico*, Bari, Laterza, 1947[4] (essays first published in 1907, 1919, 1920 and 1935).

G. Debenedetti, *Pascoli: la rivoluzione inconsapevole*, Milan, Garzanti, 1979 (lectures dating from 1953—5).

M. Valgimigli, 'Poesia e poetica di Giovanni Pascoli' in *Pascoli*, Florence, Sansoni, 1956.

G. Contini, 'Il linguaggio del Pascoli' in *Studi pascoliani*, Faenza, 1958; reproduced in vol. i of the Mondadori 'Oscar' edn. of *Poesie*, pp. xxiii—lviii.

U. Bosco, 'Il. Pascoli fra Ottocento e Novecento' in *Realismo romantico*, Palermo, Sciascia, 1959, pp. 233—50.

N. Sapegno, 'Nota sulla poesia del Pascoli' in *Pagine di storia letteraria*, Palermo, Manfredi, 1960, pp. 271—9.

F. Flora, *La poesia di Giovanni Pascoli*, Bologna, Zanichelli, 1959.

L. Anceschi, *Le poetiche del Novecento in Italia*, Turin, Paravia, 1962, 1973[4]; see Section III: 'Poetica delle cose ed estetismo', pp. 65—74.

G. Petrocchi, *Pascoli*, Turin, Edizioni RAI, 1962.

E. Sanguineti, *Ideologia e linguaggio*, Milan, Feltrinelli, 1965, 1970[2], pp. 7—37.

C. Distante, *Giovanni Pascoli poeta inquieto tra '800 e '900*, Florence, Olschki, 1968.

C. F. Goffis, 'Le strutture pascoliane' and 'La dissoluzione dell'ordine gnoseologico' in *Pascoli antico e nuovo*, Brescia, Paideia Editrice, 1969, pp. 17—73.

C. Colicchi, *Giovanni Pascoli* (Introduzione e guida... con una presentazione del Decadentismo), Florence, Le Monnier, 1970.

G. L. Beccaria, *Metrica e sintassi nella poesia di Giovanni Pascoli*, Turin, Giappichelli, 1970.

E. Gioanola, *La poesia del Decadentismo: Pascoli e d'Annunzio*, Turin, Società Editrice Internazionale, 1972.

G. Trombatore, *Memoria e simbolo nella poesia di Giovanni Pascoli*, Reggio Calabria, Parallelo 38, 1975.

L. M. Marchetti, Introduction to *Pascoli: testi e commento*, Marietti edd., 1976.

SELECTED POEMS

MYRICAE

1 Alba festiva

Che hanno le campane,
che squillano vicine,
che ronzano lontane?

È un inno senza fine,
5 or d'oro, ora d'argento,
nell'ombre mattutine.

Con un dondolío lento
implori, o voce d'oro,
nel cielo sonnolento.

10 Tra il cantico sonoro
il tuo tintinno squilla,
voce argentina — Adoro,

adoro — Dilla, dilla,
la nota d'oro — L'onda
15 pende dal ciel, tranquilla.

Ma voce piú profonda
sotto l'amor rimbomba,
par che al desío risponda:

la voce della tomba.

2 Speranze e memorie

Paranzelle in alto mare
bianche bianche,

io vedeva palpitare
come stanche:
5   o speranze, ale di sogni
per il mare!

Volgo gli occhi; e credo in cielo
rivedere
paranzelle sotto un velo,
10 nere nere:
o memorie, ombre di sogni
per il cielo!

3 Allora

Allora... in un tempo assai lunge
felice fui molto; non ora:
ma quanta dolcezza mi giunge
da tanta dolcezza d'allora!

5   Quell'anno! per anni che poi
fuggirono, che fuggiranno,
non puoi, mio pensiero, non puoi,
portare con te, che quell'anno!

Un giorno fu quello, ch'è senza
10 compagno, ch'è senza ritorno;
la vita fu vana parvenza
sí prima sí dopo quel giorno!

Un punto!... cosí passeggero,
che in vero passò non raggiunto,
15 ma bello cosí, che molto ero
felice, felice, quel punto!

4 Patria

Sogno d'un dí d'estate.

Quanto scampanellare
tremulo di cicale!
Stridule pel filare
5   moveva il maestrale
le foglie accartocciate.

Scendea tra gli olmi il sole
in fascie polverose;
erano in ciel due sole
10 nuvole, tenui, róse:
due bianche spennellate

in tutto il ciel turchino.

Siepi di melograno,
fratte di tamerice,
15 il palpito lontano
d'una trebbïatrice,
l'angelus argentino ...

dov'ero? Le campane
mi dissero dov'ero,
20 piangendo, mentre un cane
latrava al forestiero,
che andava a capo chino.

5 Il nunzio

Un murmure, un rombo ...

Son solo: ho la testa
confusa di tetri
pensieri. Mi desta

5   quel murmure ai vetri.
Che brontoli, o bombo?

che nuove mi porti?

E cadono l'ore
giú giú, con un lento
10   gocciare. Nel cuore
lontane risento
parole di morti...

Che brontoli, o bombo?

che avviene nel mondo?
15   Silenzio infinito.
Ma insiste profondo,
solingo smarrito,
quel lugubre rombo.

6   La cucitrice

L'alba per la valle nera
sparpagliò le greggi bianche:
tornano ora nella sera
e s'arrampicano stanche;
5   una stella le conduce.

Torna via dalla maestra
la covata, e passa lenta:
c'è del biondo alla finestra
tra un basilico e una menta:
10   è Maria che cuce e cuce.

Per chi cuci e per che cosa?
un lenzuolo? un bianco velo?
Tutto il cielo è color rosa,
rosa e oro, e tutto il cielo

15 sulla testa le riluce.

Alza gli occhi dal lavoro:
una lagrima? un sorriso?
Sotto il cielo rosa e oro,
chini gli occhi, chino il viso,
20 ella cuce, cuce, cuce.

7 Romagna

a Severino

Sempre un villaggio, sempre una campagna
mi ride al cuore (o piange), Severino:
il paese ove, andando, ci accompagna
l'azzurra visïon di San Marino:

5 sempre mi torna al cuore il mio paese
cui regnarono Guidi e Malatesta,
cui tenne pure il Passator cortese,
re della strada, re della foresta.

Là nelle stoppie dove singhiozzando
10 va la tacchina con l'altrui covata,
presso gli stagni lustreggianti, quando
lenta vi guazza l'anatra iridata,

oh! fossi io teco; e perderci nel verde,
e di tra gli olmi, nido alle ghiandaie,
15 gettarci l'urlo che lungi si perde
dentro il meridïano ozio dell'aie;

mentre il villano pone dalle spalle
gobbe la ronca e afferra la scodella,
e 'l bue rumina nelle opache stalle
20 la sua laborïosa lupinella.

Da' borghi sparsi le campane in tanto

si rincorron coi lor gridi argentini:
chiamano al rezzo, alla quiete, al santo
desco fiorito d'occhi di bambini.

25 Già m'accoglieva in quelle ore bruciate
sotto ombrello di trine una mimosa,
che fioria la mia casa ai dí d'estate
co' suoi pennacchi di color di rosa;

e s'abbracciava per lo sgretolato
30 muro un folto rosaio a un gelsomino;
guardava il tutto un pioppo alto e slanciato,
chiassoso a giorni come un birichino.

Era il mio nido: dove, immobilmente,
io galoppava con Guidon Selvaggio
35 e con Astolfo; o mi vedea presente
l'imperatore nell'eremitaggio.

E mentre aereo mi poneva in via
con l'ippogrifo pel sognato alone,
o risonava nella stanza mia
40 muta il dettare di Napoleone;

udia tra i fieni allor allor falciati
de' grilli il verso che perpetuo trema,
udiva dalle rane dei fossati
un lungo interminabile poema.

45 E lunghi, e interminati, erano quelli
ch'io meditai, mirabili a sognare:
stormir di frondi, cinguettío d'uccelli,
risa di donne, strepito di mare.

Ma da quel nido, rondini tardive,
50 tutti tutti migrammo un giorno nero;
io, la mia patria or è dove si vive;
gli altri son poco lungi; in cimitero.

Cosí piú non verrò per la calura
tra que' tuoi polverosi biancospini,
55 ch'io non ritrovi nella mia verzura
del cuculo ozïoso i piccolini,

Romagna solatía, dolce paese,
cui regnarono Guidi e Malatesta,
cui tenne pure il Passator cortese,
60 re della strada, re della foresta.

8   Rio Salto

Lo so: non era nella valle fonda
suon che s'udia di palafreni andanti:
era l'acqua che giú dalle stillanti
tegole a furia percotea la gronda.

5 Pur via e via per l'infinita sponda
passar vedevo i cavalieri erranti;
scorgevo le corazze luccicanti,
scorgevo l'ombra galoppar sull'onda.

Cessato il vento poi, non di galoppi
10 il suono udivo, né vedea tremando
fughe remote al dubitoso lume;

ma voi solo vedevo, amici pioppi!
Brusivano soave tentennando
lungo la sponda del mio dolce fiume.

9   I puffini dell'Adriatico

Tra cielo e mare (un rigo di carmino
recide intorno l'acque marezzate)
parlano. È un'alba cerula d'estate:

non una randa in tutto quel turchino.

5 Pur voci reca il soffio del garbino
con ozïose e tremule risate.
Sono i puffini: su le mute ondate
pende quel chiacchiericcio mattutino.

Sembra un vociare, per la calma, fioco,
10 di marinai, ch'ad ora ad ora giunga
tra 'l fievole sciacquío della risacca;

quando, stagliate dentro l'oro e il fuoco,
le paranzelle in una riga lunga
dondolano sul mar liscio di lacca.

10 Il santuario

Come un'arca d'aromi oltremarini,
il santuario, a mezzo la scogliera,
esala ancora l'inno e la preghiera
tra i lunghi intercolunnii de' pini;

5 e trema ancor de' palpiti divini
che l'hanno scosso nella dolce sera,
quando dalla grand'abside severa
uscía l'incenso in fiocchi cilestrini.

S'incurva in una luminosa arcata
10 il ciel sovr'esso: alle colline estreme
il Carro è fermo e spia l'ombra che sale.

Sale con l'ombra il suon d'una cascata
che grave nel silenzio sacro geme
con un sospiro eternamente uguale.

11 Tre versi dell'Ascreo

«Non di perenni fiumi passar l'onda,
che tu non preghi volto alla corrente
pura, e le mani tuffi nella monda
        acqua lucente»

5 dice il poeta. E cosí guarda, o saggio,
tu nel dolore, cupo fiume errante;
passa, e le mani reca dal passaggio
        sempre piú sante ...

12 Fides

Quando brillava il vespero vermiglio,
e il cipresso pareva oro, oro fino,
la madre disse al piccoletto figlio:
Cosí fatto è lassú tutto un giardino.
5 Il bimbo dorme, e sogna i rami d'oro,
gli alberi d'oro, le foreste d'oro;
mentre il cipresso nella notte nera
scagliasi al vento, piange alla bufera.

13 Ceppo

È mezzanotte. Nevica. Alla pieve
suonano a doppio; suonano l'entrata.
Va la Madonna bianca tra la neve:
spinge una porta; l'apre: era accostata.
5 Entra nella capanna: la cucina
è piena d'un sentor di medicina.
Un bricco al fuoco s'ode borbottare:
piccolo il ceppo brucia al focolare.

Un gran silenzio. Sono a messa? Bene.
10 Gesú trema; Maria si accosta al fuoco.
Ma ecco un suono, un rantolo che viene
di su, sempre piú fievole e piú roco.
Il bricco versa e sfrigge: la campana,
col vento, or s'avvicina, or s'allontana.
15 La Madonna, con una mano al cuore,
geme: Una mamma, figlio mio, che muore!

E piano piano, col suo bimbo fiso
nel ceppo, torna all'uscio, apre, s'avvia.
Il ceppo sbracia e crepita improvviso,
20 il bricco versa e sfrigola via via:
quel rantolo ... è finito. O Maria stanca!
bianca tu passi tra la neve bianca.
Suona d'intorno il doppio dell'entrata:
voce velata, malata, sognata.

14 Orfano

Lenta la neve fiocca, fiocca, fiocca.
Senti: una zana dondola pian piano.
Un bimbo piange, il piccol dito in bocca;
canta una vecchia, il mento sulla mano.
5 La vecchia canta: Intorno al tuo lettino
c'e rose e gigli, tutto un bel giardino.
Nel bel giardino il bimbo s'addormenta.
La neve fiocca lenta, lenta, lenta ...

15 Il cacciatore

Frulla un tratto l'idea nell'aria immota;
canta nel cielo. Il cacciator la vede,
l'ode; la segue: il cuor dentro gli nuota.

Se poi col dardo, come fil di sole
lucido e retto, bàttesela al piede,
oh il poeta! gioiva; ora si duole.

Deh! gola d'oro e occhi di berilli,
piccoletta del cielo alto sirena,
ecco, tu piú non voli, piú non brilli,
piú non canti: e non basti alla mia cena.

16 Arano

Al campo, dove roggio nel filare
qualche pampano brilla, e dalle fratte
sembra la nebbia mattinal fumare,

arano: a lente grida, uno le lente
vacche spinge; altri semina; un ribatte
le porche con sua marra pazïente;

ché il passero saputo in cor già gode,
e il tutto spia dai rami irti del moro;
e il pettirosso: nelle siepi s'ode
il suo sottil tintinno come d'oro.

17 Di lassú

La lodola perduta nell'aurora
si spazia, e di lassú canta alla villa,
che un fil di fumo qua e là vapora;

di lassú largamente bruni farsi
i solchi mira quella sua pupilla
lontana, e' i bianchi bovi a coppie sparsi.

Qualche zolla nel campo umido e nero
luccica al sole, netta come specchio:

fa il villano mannelle in suo pensiero,
10 e il canto del cuculo ha nell'orecchio.

18 Lavandare

Nel campo mezzo grigio e mezzo nero
resta un aratro senza buoi, che pare
dimenticato, tra il vapor leggiero.

E cadenzato dalla gora viene
5 lo sciabordare delle lavandare
con tonfi spessi e lunghe cantilene:

Il vento soffia e nevica la frasca,
e tu non torni ancora al tuo paese!
quando partisti, come son rimasta!
10 come l'aratro in mezzo alla maggese.

19 La via ferrata

Tra gli argini su cui mucche tranquilla-
mente pascono, bruna si difila
la via ferrata che lontano brilla;

e nel cielo di perla dritti, uguali,
5 con loro trama delle aeree fila
digradano in fuggente ordine i pali.

Qual di gemiti e d'ululi rombando
cresce e dilegua femminil lamento?
I fili di metallo a quando a quando
10 squillano, immensa arpa sonora, al vento.

20 Mezzogiorno

L'osteria della pergola è in faccende:
piena è di grida, di brusío, di sordi
tonfi; il camin fumante a tratti splende.

Sulla soglia, tra il nembo degli odori
5 pingui, un mendico brontola: Altri tordi
c'era una volta, e altri cacciatori.

Dice, e il cor s'è beato. Mezzogiorno
dal villaggio a rintocchi lenti squilla;
e dai remoti campanili intorno
10 un'ondata di riso empie la villa.

21 Già dalla mattina

Acqua, rimbomba; dondola, cassetta;
gira, coperchio, intorno la bronzina;
versa, tramoggia, il gran dalla bocchetta;

spolvero, svola. Nero da una fratta
5 l'asino attende già dalla mattina
presso la risonante cateratta.

Le orecchie scrolla e volgesi a guardare,
ché tardi, tra finire, andar bel bello,
intridere, spianare ed infornare,
10 sul desco fumerai, pan di cruschello.

22 Carrettiere

O carrettiere che dai neri monti
vieni tranquillo, e fosti nella notte
sotto ardue rupi, sopra aerei ponti;

     che mai diceva il querulo aquilone
5   che muggía nelle forre e fra le grotte?
     Ma tu dormivi, sopra il tuo carbone.

     A mano a mano lungo lo stradale
     venía fischiando un soffio di procella:
     ma tu sognavi ch'era di natale;
10   udivi i suoni d'una cennamella.

23 In capannello

     Cigola il lungo e tremulo cancello
     e la via sbarra; ritte allo steccato
     cianciano le comari in capannello:

     parlan d'uno ch'è un altro scrivo scrivo;
5   del vin che costa un occhio, e ce n'è stato;
     del governo; di questo mal cattivo;

     del piccino; del grande ch'è sui venti;
     del maiale, che mangia e non ingrassa –
     Nero avanti a quelli occhi indifferenti
10   il traino con fragore di tuon passa.

24 Il cane

     Noi mentre il mondo va per la sua strada,
     noi ci rodiamo, e in cuor doppio è l'affanno,
     e perché vada, e perché lento vada.

     Tal, quando passa il grave carro avanti
5   del casolare, che il rozzon normanno
     stampa il suolo con zoccoli sonanti,

     sbuca il can dalla fratta, come il vento;
     lo precorre, rincorre; uggiola, abbaia.

Il carro è dilungato lento lento.
10   Il cane torna sternutando all'aia.

25 Il mago

«Rose al verziere, rondini al verone!»

Dice, e l'aria alle sue dolci parole
sibila d'ali, e l'irta siepe fiora.
Altro il savio potrebbe; altro non vuole;
5   pago se il ciel gli canta e il suol gli odora;
suoi nunzi manda alla nativa aurora,
a biondi capi intreccia sue corone.

26 Contrasto

I

Io prendo un po' di silice e di quarzo:
lo fondo; aspiro; e soffio poi di lena:
ve' la fïala, come un dí di marzo,
azzurra e grigia, torbida e serena!
5   Un cielo io faccio con un po' dí rena
e un po' di fiato. Ammira: io son l'artista.

II

Io vo per via guardando e riguardando,
solo, soletto, muto, a capo chino:
prendo un sasso, tra mille, a quando a quando
10 lo netto, arroto, taglio, lustro, affino;
chi mi sia, non importa: ecco un rubino;
vedi un topazio; prendi un'ametista.

27 Ida e Maria

O mani d'oro, le cui tenui dita
menano i tenui fili ad escir fiori
dal bianco bisso, e sí, che la fiorita
    sembra che odori;

5 o mani d'oro, che leggiere andando,
rigasi il lin, miracolo a vederlo,
qual seccia arata nell'autunno, quando
    chioccola il merlo;

o mani d'oro, di cui l'opra alterna
10 sommessamente suona senza posa,
mentre vi mira bionde la lucerna
    silenzïosa:

or m'apprestate quel che già chiedevo
funebre panno, o tenui mani d'oro,
15 però che i morti chiamano e ch'io devo
    esser con loro.

Ma non sia raso stridulo, non sia
puro amïanto; sia di quei sinceri
teli, onde grevi a voi lasciò la pia
20   madre i forzieri:

teli, a cui molte calcole sonare
udí San Mauro e molte alate spole:
un canto a tratti n'emergea di chiare,
    lente parole:

25 teli, che a notte biancheggiar sul fieno
vidi con occhio credulo d'incanti,
ne' prati al plenilunio sereno
    riscintillanti.

28 Il vecchio dei campi

Al sole, al fuoco, sue novelle ha pronte
il bianco vecchio dalla faccia austera,
che si ricorda, solo ormai, del ponte,
          quando non c'era.

5 Racconta al sole (i buoi fumidi stanno,
fissando immoti la sua lenta fola),
come far sacca si dové, quell'anno,
          delle lenzuola.

Racconta al fuoco (sfrigola bel bello
10 un ciocco d'olmo in tanto che ragiona),
come a far erba uscisse con Rondello
          Buovo d'Antona.

29 Nella macchia

Errai nel'oblío della valle
tra ciuffi di stipe fiorite,
tra quercie rigonfie di galle;

errai nella macchia piú sola,
5 per dove tra foglie marcite
spuntava l'azzurra vïola;

errai per i botri solinghi:
la cincia vedeva dai pini:
sbuffava i suoi piccoli ringhi
10   argentini.

Io siedo invisibile e solo
tra monti e foreste: la sera
non freme d'un grido, d'un volo.

Io siedo invisibile e fosco;

15 ma un cantico di capinera
   si leva dal tacito bosco.

   E il cantico all'ombre segrete
   per dove invisibile io siedo,
   con voce di flauto ripete,
20   *Io ti vedo!*

30 Dall'argine

   Posa il meriggio su la prateria.
   Non ala orma ombra nell'azzurro e verde.
   Un fumo al sole biancica: via via
              fila e si perde.

5 Ho nell'orecchio un turbinío di squilli,
   forse campani di lontana mandra;
   e, tra l'azzurro penduli, gli strilli
              della calandra.

31 Temporale

   Un bubbolío lontano . . .

   Rosseggia l'orizzonte,
   come affocato, a mare;
   nero di pece, a monte,
5 stracci di nubi chiare:
   tra il nero un casolare:
   un'ala di gabbiano.

32 Dopo l'acquazzone

   Passò strosciando e sibilando il nero

nembo: or la chiesa squilla; il tetto, rosso,
luccica; un fresco odor dal cimitero
  viene, di bosso.

5 Presso la chiesa; mentre la sua voce
tintinna, canta, a onde lunghe romba;
ruzza uno stuolo, ed alla grande croce
  tornano a bomba.

Un vel di pioggia vela l'orizzonte;
10 ma il cimitero, sotto il ciel sereno,
placido olezza: va da monte a monte
  l'arcobaleno.

33 Pioggia

Cantava al buio d'aia in aia il gallo.

E gracidò nel bosco la cornacchia:
il sole si mostrava a finestrelle.
Il sol dorò la nebbia della macchia,
5 poi si nascose; e piovve a catinelle.
Poi fra il cantare delle raganelle
guizzò sui campi un raggio lungo e giallo.

Stupíano i rondinotti dell'estate
di quel sottile scendere di spille:
10 era un brusío con languide sorsate
e chiazze larghe e picchi a mille a mille;
poi singhiozzi, e gocciar rado di stille:
di stille d'oro in coppe di cristallo.

34 Novembre

Gemmea l'aria, il sole cosí chiaro

che tu ricerchi gli albicocchi in fiore,
e del prunalbo l'odorino amaro
   senti nel cuore ...

5 Ma secco è il pruno, e le stecchite piante
di nere trame segnano il sereno,
e vuoto il cielo, e cavo al piè sonante
   sembra il terreno.

Silenzio, intorno: solo, alle ventate,
10 odi lontano, da giardini ed orti,
di foglie un cader fragile. È l'estate,
   fredda, dei morti.

35 Lo stornello

— Sospira e piange, e bagna le lenzuola
la bella figlia, quando rifà il letto, —
tale alcuno comincia un suo rispetto:
trema nell'aurea notte ogni parola;

5 e sfiora i bossi, quasi arguta spola,
l'aura con un bruire esile e schietto:
— e si rimira il suo candido petto,
e le rincresce avere a dormir sola. —

Solo, là dalla siepe, è il casolare;
10 nel casolare sta la bianca figlia;
la bianca figlia il puro ciel rimira.

Lo vuole, a stella a stella, essa contare;
ma il ciel cammina, e la brezza bisbiglia,
e quegli canta, e il cuor piange e sospira.

36 Benedizione

È la sera: piano piano
passa il prete pazïente,
salutando della mano
ciò che vede e ciò che sente.

5 Tutti e tutto il buon piovano
benedice santamente:
anche il loglio, là, nel grano;
qua, ne' fiori, anche il serpente.

Ogni ramo, ogni uccellino
10 sí del bosco e sí del tetto,
nel passare ha benedetto:

anche il falco, anche il falchetto
nero in mezzo al ciel turchino,
anche il corvo, anche il becchino,
15   poverino,

che lassú nel cimitero
raspa raspa il giorno intiero.

37 Con gli angioli

Erano in fiore i lilla e l'ulivelle;
  ella cuciva l'abito di sposa:

né l'aria ancora apría bocci di stelle,
  né s'era chiusa foglia di mimosa:

5 quand'ella rise; rise, o rondinelle
  nere, improvvisa: ma con chi? di cosa?

rise, cosí, con gli angioli; con quelle
  nuvole d'oro, nuvole di rosa.

38 Mare

M'affaccio alla finestra, e vedo il mare:
vanno le stelle, tremolano l'onde.
Vedo stelle passare, onde passare:
un guizzo chiama, un palpito risponde.

5   Ecco sospira l'acqua, alita il vento:
sul mare è apparso un bel ponte d'argento.

Ponte gettato sui laghi sereni,
per chi dunque sei fatto e dove meni?

39 Il nido

Dal selvaggio rosaio scheletrito
penzola un nido. Come, a primavera,
ne prorompeva empiendo la riviera
il cinguettío del garrulo convito!

5   Or v'è sola una piuma, che all'invito
dèl vento esita, palpita leggiera;
qual sogno antico in anima severa,
fuggente sempre e non ancor fuggito:

e già l'occhio dal cielo ora si toglie;
10 dal cielo dove un ultimo concento
salí raggiando e dileguò nell'aria;

e si figge alla terra, in cui le foglie
putride stanno, mentre a onde il vento
piange nella campagna solitaria.

40 Il lampo

E cielo e terra si mostrò qual era:

la terra ansante, livida, in sussulto;
il cielo ingombro, tragico, disfatto:
bianca bianca nel tacito tumulto
5 una casa apparí sparí d'un tratto;
come un occhio, che, largo, esterrefatto,
s'aprí si chiuse, nella notte nera.

41 Il tuono

E nella notte nera come il nulla,

a un tratto, col fragor d'arduo dirupo
che frana, il tuono rimbombò di schianto:
rimbombò, rimbalzò, rotolò cupo,
5 e tacque, e poi rimareggiò rinfranto,
e poi vaní. Soave allora un canto
s'udí di madre, e il moto di una culla.

42 La baia tranquilla

Getta l'ancora, amor mio;
non un'onda in questa baia.
Quale assiduo sciacquío
fanno l'acque tra la ghiaia!

5 Vien dal lido solatío,
vien di là dalla giuncaia,
lungo vien, come un addio,
un cantar di marinaia.

Tra le vetrici e gli ontani
10 vedi un fiume luccicare;
uno stormo di gabbiani

nel turchino biancheggiare;

e sul poggio, piú lontani,
i cipressi neri stare.

15   Mare! mare!
dolce là, dal poggio azzurro,
il tuo urlo e il tuo sussurro.

43 La Sirena

La sera, fra il sussurrío lento
dell'acqua che succhia la rena,
dal mare nebbioso un lamento
si leva: il tuo canto, o Sirena.

5 E sembra che salga, che salga,
poi rompa in un gemito grave.
E l'onda sospira tra l'alga,
e passa una larva di nave:

un'ombra di nave che sfuma
10 nel grigio, ove muore quel grido;
che porta con sé, nella bruma,
dei cuori che tornano al lido:

al lido che fugge, che scese
già nella caligine, via;
15 che porta via tutto, le chiese
che suonano l'avemaria,

le case che su per la balza
nel grigio traspaiono appena,
e l'ombra del fumo che s'alza
20 tra forse il brusío della cena.

PRIMI POEMETTI

44 Il vischio

I

Non li ricordi piú, dunque, i mattini
meravigliosi? Nuvole a' nostri occhi,
rosee di peschi, bianche di susini,

parvero: un'aria pendula di fiocchi,
5   o bianchi o rosa, o l'uno e l'altro: meli,
floridi peri, gracili albicocchi.

Tale quell'orto ci apparí tra i veli
del nostro pianto, e tenne in sé riflessa
per giorni un'improvvisa alba dei cieli.

10   Era, sai, la speranza e la promessa,
quella; ma l'ape da' suoi bugni uscita
pasceva già l'illusïone; ond'essa

fa, come io faccio, il miele di sua vita.

II

Una nube, una pioggia ... a poco a poco
15   tornò l'inverno; e noi sentimmo, chiusi
per lunghi giorni, brontolare il fuoco.

Sparvero i bianchi e rossi alberi, infusi
dentro il nebbione; e per il cielo smorto
era un assiduo sibilo di fusi;

20   e piovve e piovve. Il sole (onde mai sorto?)
brillò di nuovo al suon delle campane:
tutto era verde, verde era quell'orto.

Dove le branche pari a filigrane?
Tutti i petali a terra. E su l'aurora
noi calpestammo le memorie vane

ognuna con la sua lagrima ancora.

III

Ricordi? Io dissi: «O anima sorella,
vivono! E tu saprai che per la vita
si getta qualche cosa anche piú bella

della vita: la sua lieve fiorita
d'ali. La pianta che a' suoi rami vede
i mille pomi sizïenti, addita

per terra i fiori che all'oblío già diede...
Non però questa (io m'interruppi), questa
che non ha frutti ai rami e fiori al piede».

Stava senza timore e senza festa,
e senza inverni e senza primavere,
quella; cui non avrebbe la tempesta

tolto che foglie, nate per cadere.

IV

Albero ignoto! (io dissi: non ricordi?)
albero strano, che nel tuo fogliame
mostri due verdi e un gialleggiar discordi;

albero tristo, ch'hai diverse rame,
foglie diverse, ottuse queste, acute
quelle, e non so che rei glomi e che trame;

albero infermo della tua salute,
albero che non hai gemme fiorite,
albero che non vedi ali cadute;

albero morto, che non curi il mite

50 soffio che reca il polline, né il fischio
    del nembo che flagella aspro la vite ...

    ah! sono in te le radiche del vischio!

V

    Qual vento d'odio ti portò, qual forza
    cieca o nemica t'inserí quel molle
55 piccolo seme nella dura scorza?
    Tu non sapevi o non credevi: ei volle:
    ti solcò tutto con sue verdi vene,
    fimo si fece delle tue midolle!

    E tu languivi; e la bellezza e il bene
60 t'uscía di mente, né pulsar piú fuori
    gemme sentivi di tra il tuo lichene.

    E crebbe e vinse; e tutti i tuoi colori,
    tutte le tue soavità, col suco
    de' tuoi pomi e il profumo de' tuoi fiori,

65 sono una perla pallida di muco.

VI

    Due anime in te sono, albero. Senti
    piú la lor pugna, quando mai t'affisi
    nell'ozïoso mormorio dei venti?

    Quella che aveva lagrime e sorrisi,
70 che ti ridea col labbro de' bocciuoli,
    che ti piangea dai palmiti recisi,

    e che d'amore abbrividiva ai voli
    d'api villose, già sé stessa ignora.
    Tu vivi l'altra, e sempre piú t'involi

75 da te, fuggendo immobilmente; ed ora
    l'ombra straniera è già di te piú forte,

piú te. Sei tu, checché gemmasti allora,

ch'ora distilli il glutine di morte.

45 Digitale purpurea

I

Siedono. L'una guarda l'altra. L'una
esile e bionda, semplice di vesti
e di sguardi; ma l'altra, esile e bruna,

l'altra . . . I due occhi semplici e modesti
5   fissano gli altri due ch'ardono. «E mai
non ci tornasti?» «Mai!» «Non le vedesti

piú?» «Non piú, cara.» «Io sí: ci ritornai;
e le rividi le mie bianche suore,
e li rivissi i dolci anni che sai;

10 quei piccoli anni cosí dolci al cuore . . .»
L'altra sorrise. «E di': non lo ricordi
quell'orto chiuso? i rovi con le more?

i ginepri tra cui zirlano i tordi?
i bussi amari? quel segreto canto
15 misterioso, con quel fiore, *fior di* . . .?»

«*morte*: sí, cara.» «Ed era vero? Tanto
io ci credeva che non mai, Rachele,
sarei passata al triste fiore accanto.

Ché si diceva: il fiore ha come un miele
20 che inebria l'aria: un suo vapor che bagna
l'anima d'un oblío dolce e crudele.

Oh! quel convento in mezzo alla montagna
cerulea!» Maria parla: una mano
posa su quella della sua compagna;

25 e l'una e l'altra guardano lontano.

II

Vedono. Sorge nell'azzurro intenso
del ciel di maggio il loro monastero,
pieno di litanie, pieno d'incenso.

Vedono; e si profuma il lor pensiero
30 d'odor di rose e di viole a ciocche,
di sentor d'innocenza e di mistero.

E negli orecchi ronzano, alle bocche
salgono melodie, dimenticate,
là, da tastiere appena appena tocche...

35 Oh! quale vi sorrise oggi, alle grate,
ospite caro? onde piú rosse e liete
tornaste alle sonanti camerate

oggi: ed oggi, piú alto, *Ave*, ripete,
Ave Maria, la vostra voce in coro;
40 e poi d'un tratto (perché mai?) piangete...

Piangono, un poco, nel tramonto d'oro,
senza perché. Quante fanciulle sono
nell'orto, bianco qua e là di loro!

Bianco e ciarliero. Ad or ad or, col suono
45 di vele al vento, vengono. Rimane
qualcuna, e legge in un suo libro buono.

In disparte da loro agili e sane,
una spiga di fiori, anzi di dita
spruzzolate di sangue, dita umane,

50 l'alito ignoto spande di sua vita.

III

«Maria!» «Rachele!» Un poco piú le mani

si premono. In quell'ora hanno veduto
la fanciullezza, i cari anni lontani.

Memorie (l'una sa dell'altra al muto
55 premere) dolci, come è tristo e pio
il lontanar d'un ultimo saluto!

«Maria!» «Rachele!» Questa piange, «Addio!»
dice tra sé, poi volta la parola
grave a Maria, ma i neri occhi no: «Io,»

60 mormora, «sí: sentii quel fiore. Sola
ero con le cetonie verdi. Il vento
portava odor di rose e di viole a

ciocche. Nel cuore, il languido fermento
d'un sogno che notturno arse e che s'era
65 all'alba, nell'ignara anima, spento.

Maria, ricordo quella grave sera.
L'aria soffiava luce di baleni
silenzïosi. M'inoltrai leggiera,

cauta, su per i molli terrapieni
70 erbosi. I piedi mi tenéa la folta
erba. Sorridi? E dirmi sentia: Vieni!

Vieni! E fu molta la dolcezza! molta!
tanta, che, vedi... (l'altra lo stupore
alza degli occhi, e vede ora, ed ascolta

75 con un suo lungo brivido...) si muore!»

46 Suor Virginia

I

Tum tum... tum tum... — Ell'era stata in chiesa
a pregar sola, a dir la sua corona

sotto la sola lampadina accesa.

Avea chiesto pèrdono a chi perdona
5 tutto, di nulla; simile ad ancella
ch'ha gli occhi in mano della sua padrona;

a una che su l'uscio di sorella
ricca, socchiuso, prega piano, a volo;
ch'altri non oda. Era tornata in cella.

10 E ora avanti il Cristo morto solo,
avanti l'agonia di Santa Rita,
si toglieva il suo velo, il suo soggólo.

Il cingolo a tre nodi dalla vita
poi si scioglieva; un giallo teschio d'osso
15 girò tre volte nelle ceree dita.

Tum tum . . . — Chi picchia? Si rimise in dosso
lo scapolare. Forse alla parete
dell'altra stanza. L'uscio non s'è mosso.

Forse qualche educanda. Una ch'ha sete,
20 ch'ha male . . . Aprí soavemente l'uscio.
Entrò. Niente. I capelli nella rete,

le braccia in croce, gli occhi nel lor guscio . . .

II

dormivano, composte, accomodate,
le due bambine. Aperta la finestra
25 era a una gran serenità d'estate.

L'avea lasciata aperta la maestra
per via del caldo. Un alito di vento
recava odor d'acacia e di ginestra.

Ma che frufrú nell'orto del convento!
30 Passava, ora d'un gufo, ora d'un gatto,
un sordo sgnaulío subito spento.

Un grillo ora trillava, ora d'un tratto
taceva: come? Come se lí presso
fosse venuto chi sa chi, d'appiatto.

35 Un fischiettare, un camminar represso,
un raspare, un frugare, uno sfrascare
improvviso su su per il cipresso ...

Brillavan qua e là lucciole rare,
come spiando. Un ululo ogni tanto
40 veniva da un lontano casolare.

L'urlo d'un cane alla catena, e il canto
piú lontano d'un rauco vagabondo,
nell'alta notte, era la gioia e il pianto

che al monastero pervenía, dal mondo.

III

45 Dormivano. Sí: anche la sorella
piccina. Era composta, era coperta.
Suor Virginia tornò nella sua cella.

Tornò lasciando la finestra aperta
a quel lontano canto, a quel lontano
50 *bau bau* di cane ch'era sempre all'erta;

aperta a quello scalpicciar pian piano
d'uomini o foglie, a quel trillar d'un grillo,
che poi taceva sotto un piede umano ...

Dormivano. Il lor cuore era tranquillo.
55 La suora si svestí, cosí leggiera,
ch'udí per terra il picchio d'uno spillo.

S'addormentava. — *Tum tum tum...* — Che era?
E Suor Virginia si levò seduta
sul letto, mormorando una preghiera.

60　Ella ascoltò: la piccola battuta
venía di là. Si mise anche una volta
lo scapolare. Entrò. Riguardò muta.

No. L'una e l'altra si tenea raccolta
al dolce sonno. Non avean bisogno
65　di lei. La bimba s'era, sí, rivolta

sul cuore; all'altra; a ragionarci in sogno.

IV

Tornò, comprese. Avea bussato il Santo.
Era venuto il tempo di lasciare
il suo cantuccio in questa Val di pianto.

70　A quel Santo ogni sera essa all'altare
dicea tre *pater*. Egli non ignora
nell'ampia terra il nostro limitare.

Poi ch'egli va, pascendo il gregge ancora,
come allora: e devía dalla sua strada
75　per dire a questo o quello ospite: «È l'ora».

Egli è notturno come la rugiada.
E viene, e bussa fin che il sonnolento
pellegrino non s'alza e non gli bada.

Egli era, dunque, entrato nel convento
80　per rivelarle l'ora del trapasso
Picchiò. Poi stava ad aspettare attento.

Ella sentito non ne aveva il passo,
perché va scalzo. Sulla soglia trita
certo aspettava col cappuccio basso.

85　Suor Virginia il fardello della vita
doveva fare: il cielo era già rosso:
il suo fardello. Tra le ceree dita

prese il rosario col suo teschio d'osso.

V

E vennero le morte undicimila
90 vergini, con le lampade fornite
d'olio odoroso; camminando in fila;

·di bianco lino, come lei, vestite;
nelle pallide conche d'alabastro
portando accese le lor dolci vite;

95 passando, sí che in breve erano un nastro
bianco, ondeggiante, a un alito, pian piano,
nel cielo azzurro tra la terra e un astro;

passando, come gli Ave a grano a grano
d'una corona. E le dicean parole
100 di sotto il giglio che teneano in mano.

Aveva ognuna, su le bianche stole,
l'orma di sangue della sua tortura.
Anch'ella, al cuore. Le dicean: «Non duole».

Era, la prima d'esse, Ursula pura,
105 lassú, che tuttavia lampade accese
splendeano in fila per la terra oscura.

Le vergini non tutte erano ascese.
Quella picchiò tre volte con lo stelo
del giglio. E in terra Suor Virginia intese

110 quei colpettini al grande uscio del cielo.

VI

Tum tum ... — Di là, con tutto quel gran cielo
alla finestra, oh! trema come foglia
secca che prilla intorno a un ragnatelo,

la bimba, e bussa, e par ch'ora, sí, voglia
115 dirglielo: «Madre, c'è uno laggiú:
chiuda!» E volge gli aperti occhi alla soglia

dell'uscio: aspetta. Ella non venne piú.

47 La quercia caduta

Dov'era l'ombra, or sé la quercia spande
morta, né piú coi turbini tenzona.
La gente dice: Or vedo: era pur grande!

Pendono qua e là dalla corona
5   i nidïetti della primavera.
Dice la gente: Or vedo: era pur buona!

Ognuno loda, ognuno taglia. A sera
ognuno col suo grave fascio va.
Nell'aria, un pianto . . . d'una capinera

10   che cerca il nido che non troverà.

48 La siepe

I

Siepe del mio campetto, utile e pia,
che al campo sei come l'anello al dito,
che dice mia la donna che fu mia

(ch'io pur ti sono florido marito,
5   o bruna terra ubbidïente, che ami
chi ti piagò col vomero brunito . . .);

siepe che il passo chiudi co' tuoi rami
irsuti al ladro dormi 'l-dí; ma dài
ricetto ai nidi e pascolo a gli sciami;

10   siepe che rinforzai, che ripiantai,
quando crebbe famiglia, a mano a mano,
piú lieto sempre e non piú ricco mai;

d'albaspina, marruche e melograno,
tra cui la madreselva odorerà;
15 io per te vivo libero e sovrano,

verde muraglia della mia città.

II

Oh! tu sei buona! Ha sete il passeggero;
e tu cedi i tuoi chicchi alla sua sete,
ma salvi il frutto pendulo del pero.

20 Nulla fornisci alle anfore segrete
della massaia: ma per te, felice
ella i ciliegi popolosi miete.

Nulla tu rendi; ma la vite dice;
quando la poto all'orlo della strada,
25 che si sente il cucúlo alla pendice,

dice: — Il padre tu sei che, se t'aggrada,
sí mi correggi e guidi per il pioppo;
ma la siepe è la madre che mi bada. —

— Per lei vino ho nel tino, olio nel coppo —
30 rispondo. I galli plaudono dall'aia;
e lieto il cane, che non è di troppo,

ch'è la tua voce, o muta siepe, abbaia.

III

E tu pur, siepe, immobile al confine,
tu parli; breve parli tu, ché, fuori,
35 dici un divieto acuto come spine;

dentro, un assenso bello come fiori;
siepe forte ad altrui, siepe a me pia,
come la fede che donai con gli ori,

che dice mia la donna che fu mia.

49 Nella nebbia

E guardai nella valle: era sparito
tutto! sommerso! Era un gran mare piano,
grigio, senz'onde, senza lidi, unito.

E c'era appena, qua e là, lo strano
5 vocío di gridi piccoli e selvaggi:
uccelli spersi per quel mondo vano.

E alto, in cielo, scheletri di faggi,
come sospesi, e sogni di rovine
e di silenzïosi eremitaggi.

10 Ed un cane uggiolava senza fine,
né seppi donde, forse a certe péste
che sentii, né lontane né vicine;

eco di péste né tarde né preste,
alterne, eterne. E io laggiú guardai:
15 nulla ancora e nessuno, occhi, vedeste.

Chiesero i sogni di rovine: — Mai
non giungerà? — Gli scheletri di piante
chiesero: — E tu chi sei, che sempre vai? —

Io, forse, un'ombra vidi, un'ombra errante
20 con sopra il capo un largo fascio. Vidi,
e piú non vidi, nello stesso istante.

Sentii soltanto gl'inquïeti gridi
d'uccelli spersi, l'uggiolar del cane,
e, per il mar senz'onde e senza lidi,

25 le péste né vicine né lontane.

50 Il libro

I

Sopra il leggío di quercia è nell'altana,
aperto, il libro. Quella quercia ancora,
esercitata dalla tramontana,

viveva nella sua selva sonora;
5   e quel libro era antico. Eccolo: aperto,
sembra che ascolti il tarlo che lavora.

E sembra ch'uno (donde mai? non, certo,
dal tremulo uscio, cui tentenna il vento
delle montagne e il vento del deserto,

10 sorti d'un tratto . . .) sia venuto, e lento
sfogli — se n'ode il crepitar leggiero —
le carte. E l'uomo non vedo io: lo sento,

invisibile, là, come il pensiero . . .

II

Un uomo è là, che sfoglia dalla prima
15 carta all'estrema, rapido, e pian piano
va, dall'estrema, a ritrovar la prima.

E poi nell'ira del cercar suo vano
volta i fragili fogli a venti, a trenta,
a cento, con l'impaziënte mano.

20 E poi li volge a uno a uno, lenta-
mente, esitando; ma via via piú forte,
piú presto, i fogli contro i fogli avventa.

Sosta . . . Trovò? Non gemono le porte
piú, tutto oscilla in un silenzio austero.
25 Legge? . . . Un istante; e volta le contorte

pagine, e torna ad inseguire il vero.

III

E sfoglia ancora; al vespro, che da nere
nubi rosseggia; tra un errar di tuoni,
tra un alïare come di chimere.

30 E sfoglia ancora, mentre i padiglioni
tumidi al vento l'ombra tende, e viene
con le deserte costellazïoni

la sacra notte. Ancora e sempre: bene
io n'odo il crepito arido tra canti
35 lunghi nel cielo come di sirene.

Sempre. Io lo sento, tra le voci erranti,
invisibile, là, come il pensiero,
che sfoglia, avanti indietro, indietro avanti,

sotto le stelle, il libro del mistero.

51 Il transito

Il cigno canta. In mezzo delle lame
rombano le sue voci lunghe e chiare,
come percossi cembali di rame.

È l'infinita tenebra polare.
5 Grandi montagne d'un eterno gelo
póntano sopra il lastrico del mare.

Il cigno canta; e lentamente il cielo
sfuma nel buio, e si colora in giallo;
spunta una luce verde a stelo a stelo.

10 Come arpe qua e là tocche, il metallo
di quella voce tíntina; già sfiora
la verde luce i picchi di cristallo.

E nella notte, che ne trascolora,
un immenso iridato arco sfavilla,
15 e i portici profondi apre l'aurora.

L'arco verde e vermiglio arde, zampilla,
a frecce, a fasci; e poi palpita, frana
tacitamente, e riascende e brilla.

Col suono d'un rintocco di campana
20 che squilli ultimo, il cigno agita l'ale:
l'ale grandi grandi apre, e s'allontana

candido, nella luce boreale.

NUOVI POEMETTI

52 La pecorella smarrita

I

«Frate,» una voce gli diceva: «è l'ora
che tu ti svegli. Alzati! La rugiada
è sulle foglie, e viene già l'aurora».

Egli si alzava. «L'ombra si dirada
5 nel cielo. Il cielo scende a goccia a goccia.
Biancica, in terra, qua e là, la strada».

S'incamminava. «Spunta dalla roccia
un lungo stelo. In cima dello stelo,
grave di guazza pende il fiore in boccia».

10 S'inginocchiava. «Si dirompe il cielo!
Albeggia Dio! Plaudite con le mani,
pini de l'Hermon, cedri del Carmelo!»

Tre volte il gallo battea l'ali. I cani
squittíano in sogno. Le sei ali in croce
15 egli vedea di seraphim lontani.

Sentiva in cuore il rombo della voce.
Su lui, con le infinite stelle, lento,
fluiva il cielo verso la sua foce.

Era il dí del Signore, era l'avvento.
20 Spariva sotto i baratri profondi
colmi di stelle il tacito convento.

Mucchi di stelle, grappoli di mondi,
nebbie di cosmi. Il frate disse: «O duce

di nostra casa, vieni! Eccoci mondi».

25 In quella immensa polvere di luce
splendeano, occhi di draghi e di leoni,
Vega, Deneb, Aldebaran, Polluce...

E il frate udí, fissando i milïoni
d'astri, il vagito d'un agnello sperso
30 là tra le grandi costellazïoni

nella profondità dell'Universo...

II

E il dubbio entrò nel cuore tristo e pio.
«Che sei tu, Terra, perché in te si sveli
tutto il mistero, e vi s'incarni Dio?

35 O Terra, l'uno tu non sei, che i Cieli
sian l'altro! Non, del tuo Signor, sei l'orto
con astri a fiori, e lunghi sguardi a steli!

Noi ti sappiamo. Non sei, Terra, il porto
del mare in cui gli eterni astri si cullano...
40 un astro sei, senza piú luce, morto:

foglia secca d'un gruppo cui trastulla
il vento eterno in mezzo all'infinito:
scheggia, grano, favilla, atomo, nulla!»

Cosí pensava: al sommo del suo dito
45 giungeva allora da una stella il raggio
che da piú di mille anni era partito.

E vide una fiammella in un villaggio
lontano, a quelle di lassú confusa:
udí lontano un dolce suon selvaggio.

50 Laggiú da una capanna semichiusa
veniva il suono per la notte pura,
il dolce suono d'una cornamusa.

E risonava tutta la pianura
d'uno scalpiccio verso la capanna:
55 forse pastori dalla lor pastura.

E il frate al suono dell'agreste canna
ripensò quelle tante pecorelle
che il pastor buono non di lor s'affanna:

tra i fuochi accesi stanno in pace, quelle,
60 sicure là su la montagna bruna;
e il pastor buono al lume delle stelle

quaggiú ne cerca intanto una, sol una...

III

«Sei tu quell'una, tu quell'una, o Terra!
Sola, del santo monte, ove s'uccida,
65 dove sia l'odio, dove sia la guerra;

dove di tristi lagrime s'intrida
il pan di vita! Tu non sei che pianto
versato in vano! Sangue sei, che grida!

E tu volesti Dio per te soltanto:
70 volesti che scendesse sconosciuto
nell'alta notte dal suo monte santo.

Tu lo volesti in forma d'un tuo bruto
dal mal pensiero: e in una croce infame
l'alzasti in vista del suo cielo muto».

75 In cielo e in terra tremulo uno sciame
era di luci. Andavano al lamento
della zampogna, e fasci avean di strame.

Ma il frate, andando, con un pio sgomento
toccava appena la rea terra, appena
80 guardava il folgorío del firmamento:

quella nebbia di mondi, quella rena
di Soli sparsi intorno alla Polare
dentro la solitudine serena.

Ognun dei Soli nel tranquillo andare
85 traeva seco i placidi pianeti
come famiglie intorno al focolare:

oh! tutti savi, tutti buoni, queti,
persino ignari, colassú, del male,
che no, non s'ama, anche se niun lo vieti.

90 Sonava la zampogna pastorale.
E Dio scendea la cerula pendice
cercando in fondo dell'abisso astrale

la Terra, sola rea, sola infelice.

CANTI DI CASTELVECCHIO

53 La poesia

I

Io sono una lampada ch'arda
    soave!
la lampada, forse, che guarda,
pendendo alla fumida trave,
5   la veglia che fila;

e ascolta novelle e ragioni
    da bocche
celate nell'ombra, ai cantoni,
là dietro le soffici rócche
10   che albeggiano in fila:

ragioni, novelle, e saluti
d'amore, all'orecchio, confusi:
gli assidui bisbigli perduti
nel sibilo assiduo dei fusi;
15 le vecchie parole sentite
da presso con palpiti nuovi,
tra il sordo rimastico mite
    dei bovi:

II

la lampada, forse, che a cena
20   raduna;
che sboccia sul bianco, e serena
su l'ampia tovaglia sta, luna
    su prato di neve;

　　　　e arride al giocondo convito;
25　　　　　poi cenna,
　　　　d'un tratto, ad un piccolo dito,
　　　　là, nero tuttor della penna
　　　　　che corre e che beve:

　　　　ma lascia nell'ombra, alla mensa,
30　　　la madre, nel tempo ch'esplora
　　　　la figlia piú grande che pensa
　　　　guardando il mio raggio d'aurora:
　　　　rapita nell'aurea mia fiamma
　　　　non sente lo sguardo tuo vano;
35　　　già fugge, è già, povera mamma,
　　　　　lontano!

III

　　　　Se già non la lampada io sia,
　　　　　che oscilla
　　　　davanti a una dolce Maria,
40　　　vivendo dell'umile stilla
　　　　　di cento capanne:

　　　　raccolgo l'uguale tributo
　　　　　d'ulivo
　　　　da tutta la villa, e il saluto
45　　　del colle sassoso e del rivo
　　　　　sonante di canne:

　　　　e incende, il mio raggio, di sera,
　　　　tra l'ombra di mesta vïola,
　　　　nel ciglio che prega e dispera,
50　　　la povera lagrima sola;
　　　　e muore, nei lucidi albori,
　　　　tremando, il mio pallido raggio,
　　　　tra cori di vergini e fiori
　　　　　di maggio:

IV

55 o quella, velata, che al fianco
    t'addita
la donna piú bianca del bianco
lenzuolo, che in grembo, assopita,
    matura il tuo seme;

60 o quella che irraggia una cuna
    — la barca
che, alzando il fanal di fortuna,
nel mare dell'essere varca,
    si dondola, e geme —;

65 o quella che illumina tacita
tombe profonde — con visi
scarniti di vecchi; tenaci
di vergini bionde sorrisi;
tua madre!... nell'ombra senz'ore,
70 per te, dal suo triste riposo,
congiunge le mani al suo cuore
    già róso! —.

V

Io sono la lampada ch'arde
    soave!
75 nell'ore piú sole e piú tarde,
nell'ombra piú mesta, piú grave,
    piú buona, o fratello!

Ch'io penda sul capo a fanciulla
    che pensa,
80 su madre che prega, su culla
che piange, su garrula mensa,
    su tacito avello;

lontano risplende l'ardore
mio casto all'errante che trita

85 notturno, piangendo nel cuore,
la pallida via della vita:
s'arresta; ma vede il mio raggio,
che gli arde nell'anima blando:
riprende l'oscuro vïaggio
90   cantando.

54 Il compagno dei taglialegna

I

Nel bosco, qua e là, lombardi
    sono taciti al lavoro.

Dall'alba s'ode sino a tardi
    sci e *sci* e *sci* e *sci* ...

5 È oltre mare l'Alpe loro,
    mare, donde nasce il dí.

II

A due a due: l'uno tra il vento,
    l'altro, inginocchiato in faccia.

Da basso il vecchio bianco e scento,
10   in alto la gioventú.

E forza con le forti braccia!
    Su e giú, e su e giú.

III

Con loro c'è il pittiere solo,
    ora in terra, ora sul ramo.

15 Fa un salto, un frullo, un giro, un volo;
    molleggia, piú qui, piú lí:

e fa sentire il suo richiamo
tra quel *sci* e *sci* e *sci* . . .

IV

Il Santo aveva da piombare
un bel toppo di cipresso.

Maria restava al focolare
che dava latte a Gesú.

Ora il pittiere era lí presso.
Disse il Santo: — Vien qui tu! —

V

Tuffò la spugna il Santo, ed ecco
tinse di sinopia il filo.

— Un capo tieni tu col becco —
disse al pittiere: — costí! —

Maria non piú dal dolce asilo
ora udiva *sci* . . . *sci* . . . *sci* . . .

VI

E' sdipanava col girello,
zitto, il filo per la trave.

L'aveva teso già bel bello,
stava per batterlo su . . .

Ma ecco si sentí: AVE!
Era Maria con Gesú.

VII

Il pittiere si voltò netto . . .
Torto venne il segno rosso.

La spugna gli gettò nel petto

40   San Giuseppe; e fu cosí

    che, diventato pettirosso,
        quando sente *sci* ... *sci* ... *sci* ...

VIII

    vien sempre, gira intorno al toppo,
        guarda e frulla, guarda e vola;

45   ma ora non s'accosta troppo,
        ch'ora non si fida piú:

    e col suo canto ti consola,
        povera esule tribú!

55 Nebbia

    Nascondi le cose lontane,
    tu nebbia impalpabile e scialba,
    tu fumo che ancora rampolli,
        su l'alba,
5   da' lampi notturni e da' crolli
        d'aeree frane!

    Nascondi le cose lontane,
    nascondimi quello ch'è morto!
    Ch'io veda soltanto la siepe
10   dell'orto,
    la mura ch'ha piene le crepe
        di valerïane.

    Nascondi le cose lontane:
    le cose son ebbre di pianto!
15   Ch'io veda i due peschi, i due meli,
        soltanto,
    che dànno i soavi lor mieli
        pel nero mio pane.

Nascondi le cose lontane
20 che vogliono ch'ami e che vada!
Ch'io veda là solo quel bianco
   di strada,
che un giorno ho da fare tra stanco
   don don di campane . . .

25 Nascondi le cose lontane,
nascondile, involale al volo
del cuore! Ch'io veda il cipresso
   là, solo,
qui, solo quest'orto, cui presso
30   sonnecchia il mio cane.

56 Il brivido

Mi scosse, e mi corse
le vene il ribrezzo.
Passata m'è forse
rasente, col rezzo
5 dell'ombra sua nera
la morte . . .
   Com'era?

Veduta vanita,
com'ombra di mosca:
10 ma ombra infinita,
di nuvola fosca
che tutto fa sera:
la morte . . .
   Com'era?

15 Tremenda e veloce
come un uragano
che senza una voce
dilegua via vano:

silenzio e bufera:
20 la morte...
        Com'era?

Chi vede lei, serra
né apre piú gli occhi.
Lo metton sotterra
25 che niuno lo tocchi,
gli chieda — Com'era?
rispondi...
        com'era? —

57 La voce

C'è una voce nella mia vita,
che avverto nel punto che muore;
    voce stanca, voce smarrita,
col tremito del batticuore:

5   voce d'una accorsa anelante,
che al povero petto s'afferra
    per dir tante cose e poi tante,
ma piena ha la bocca di terra:

tante tante cose che vuole
10 ch'io sappia, ricordi, sí... sí...
    ma di tante tante parole
non sento che un soffio... *Zvanî*...

Quando avevo tanto bisogno
di pane e di compassïone,
15 che mangiavo solo nel sogno,
svegliandomi al primo boccone;

    una notte, su la spalletta
del Reno, coperta di neve,
    dritto e solo (passava in fretta

20 l'acqua brontolando, Si beve?);

dritto e solo, con un gran pianto
d'avere a finire cosí,
mi sentii d'un tratto daccanto
quel soffio di voce ... *Zvaní*...

25 Oh! la terra, com'è cattiva!
la terra, che amari bocconi!
Ma voleva dirmi, io capiva:
— No ... no ... Di' le devozïoni!

Le dicevi con me pian piano,
30 con sempre la voce piú bassa:
la tua mano nella mia mano:
ridille! vedrai che ti passa.

Non far piangere piangere piangere
(ancora!) chi tanto soffrí!
35 il tuo pane, prega il tuo angelo
che te lo porti ... *Zvaní*... —

Una notte dalle lunghe ore
(nel carcere!), che all'improvviso
dissi — Avresti molto dolore,
40 tu, se non t'avessero ucciso,

ora, o babbo! — che il mio pensiero,
dal carcere, con un lamento,
vide il babbo nel cimitero,
le pie sorelline in convento:

45 e che agli uomini, la mia vita,
volevo lasciargliela lí ...
risentii la voce smarrita
che disse in un soffio ... *Zvaní*...

Oh! la terra come è cattiva!
50 non lascia discorrere, poi!

Ma voleva dirmi, io capiva:
— Piuttosto di' un requie per noi!

Non possiamo nel camposanto
piú prendere sonno un minuto,
55 ché sentiamo struggersi in pianto
le bimbe che l'hanno saputo!

Oh! la vita mia che ti diedi
per loro, lasciarla vuoi qui?
qui, mio figlio? dove non vedi
60 chi uccise tuo padre ... *Zvanî*? ... —

Quante volte sei rivenuta
nei cupi abbandoni del cuore,
voce stanca, voce perduta,
col tremito del batticuore:

65 voce d'una accorsa anelante
che ai poveri labbri si tocca
per dir tante cose e poi tante,
ma piena di terra ha la bocca:

la tua bocca! con i tuoi baci,
70 già tanto accorati a quei dí!
a quei dí beati e fugaci
che aveva i tuoi baci ... *Zvanî*! ...

che m'addormentavano gravi
campane col placido canto,
75 e sul capo biondo che amavi,
sentivo un tepore di pianto!

che ti lessi negli occhi, ch'erano
pieni di pianto, che sono
pieni di terra, la preghiera
80 di vivere e d'essere buono!

Ed allora, quasi un comando,

no, quasi un compianto, t'uscí
    la parola che a quando a quando
mi dici anche adesso . . . *Zvaní* . . .

58 Il sonnellino

Guardai, di tra l'ombra, già nera,
del sonno, smarrendo qualcosa
lí dentro: nell'aria non era
    che un cirro di rosa.

5 E il cirro dal limpido azzurro
splendeva sui grigi castelli,
levando per tutto un sussurro
    d'uccelli;

che sopra le tegole rosse
10 del tetto e su l'acque del rio
cantavano, e non che non fosse
    silenzio ed oblío:

cantavano come non sanno
cantare che i sogni nel cuore,
15 che cantano forte e non fanno
    rumore.

E io mi rivolsi nel blando
mio sonno, in un sonno di rosa,
cercando cercando cercando
20   quel vecchio qualcosa;

e forse lo vidi e lo presi,
guidato da un canto d'uccelli,
non so per che ignoti paesi
    piú belli . . .

25 che pure ravviso, e mi volgo,

piú belli, a guardarli piú buono . . .
Ma tutto mi toglie la folgore . . .
   O subito tuono!

ch'hai fatto succedere a un'alba
30 piaciuta tra il sonno, passata
nel sonno, una stridula e scialba
   giornata!

59 Il gelsomino notturno

E s'aprono i fiori notturni,
nell'ora che penso a' miei cari.
   Sono apparse in mezzo ai viburni
   le farfalle crepuscolari.

5 Da un pezzo si tacquero i gridi:
là sola una casa bisbiglia.
   Sotto l'ali dormono i nidi,
   come gli occhi sotto le ciglia.

Dai calici aperti si esala
10 l'odore di fragole rosse.
   Splende un lume là nella sala.
   Nasce l'erba sopra le fosse.

Un'ape tardiva sussurra
trovando già prese le celle.
15   La Chioccetta per l'aia azzurra
   va col suo pigolío di stelle.

Per tutta la notte s'esala
l'odore che passa col vento.
   Passa il lume su per la scala;
20   brilla al primo piano: s'è spento . . .

   È l'alba: si chiudono i petali

60 La canzone del girarrosto

I

Domenica! il dí che a mattina
sorride e sospira al tramonto!...
Che ha quella teglia in cucina?
che brontola brontola brontola...

5 È fuori un frastuono di giuoco,
per casa è un sentore di spigo...
Che ha quella pentola al fuoco?
che sfrigola sfrigola sfrigola...

E già la massaia ritorna
10   da messa;
cosí come trovasi adorna,
    s'appressa:

la brage qua copre, là desta,
passando, *frr*, come in un volo,
15 spargendo un odore di festa,
di nuovo, di tela e giaggiolo.

II

La macchina è in punto; l'agnello
nel lungo schidione è già pronto;
la teglia è sul chiuso fornello,
20 che brontola brontola brontola...

Ed ecco la macchina parte
da sé, col suo trepido intrigo:

la pentola nera è da parte,
che sfrigola sfrigola sfrigola ...

25 Ed ecco che scende, che sale,
   che frulla,
che va con un dondolo eguale
   di culla.

La legna scoppietta; ed un fioco
30 fragore all'orecchio risuona
di qualche invitato, che un poco
s'è fermo su l'uscio, e ragiona.

III

È l'ora, in cucina, che troppi
due sono, ed un solo non basta:
35 si cuoce, tra murmuri e scoppi,
la bionda matassa di pasta.

Qua, nella cucina, lo svolo
di piccole grida d'impero;
là, in sala, il ronzare, ormai solo,
40 d'un ospite molto ciarliero.

Avanti i suoi ciocchi, senz'ira
   né pena,
la docile macchina gira
   serena,

45 qual docile servo, una volta
ch'ha inteso, né altro bisogna:
lavora nel mentre che ascolta,
lavora nel mentre che sogna.

IV

Va sempre, s'affretta, ch'è l'ora,
50 con una vertigine molle:

con qualche suo fremito incuora
la pentola grande che bolle.

È l'ora: s'affretta, né tace,
ché sgrida, rimprovera, accusa,
55 col suo ticchettío pertinace,
la teglia che brontola chiusa.

Campana lontana si sente
    sonare.
Un'altra con onde piú lente,
60   piú chiare,

risponde. Ed il piccolo schiavo
già stanco, girando bel bello,
già mormora, *in tavola! in tavola!*,
e dondola il suo campanello.

61 L'ora di Barga

Al mio cantuccio, donde non sento
se non le reste brusir del grano,
il suon dell'ore viene col vento
dal non veduto borgo montano:
5 suono che uguale, che blando cade,
come una voce che persuade.

Tu dici, È l'ora; tu dici, È tardi,
voce che cadi blanda dal cielo.
Ma un poco ancora lascia che guardi
10 l'albero, il ragno, l'ape, lo stelo,
cose ch'han molti secoli o un anno
o un'ora, e quelle nubi che vanno.

Lasciami immoto qui rimanere
fra tanto moto d'ale e di fronde;
15 e udire il gallo che da un podere

chiama, e da un altro l'altro risponde,
e, quando altrove l'anima è fissa,
gli strilli d'una cincia che rissa.

E suona ancora l'ora, e mi manda
20 prima un suo grido di meraviglia
tinnulo, e quindi con la sua blanda
voce di prima parla e consiglia,
e grave grave grave m'incuora:
mi dice, È tardi; mi dice, È l'ora.

25 Tu vuoi che pensi dunque al ritorno,
voce che cadi blanda dal cielo!
Ma bello è questo poco di giorno
che mi traluce come da un velo!
Lo so ch'è l'ora, lo so ch'è tardi;
30 ma un poco ancora lascia che guardi.

Lascia che guardi dentro il mio cuore,
lascia ch'io viva del mio passato;
se c'è sul bronco sempre quel fiore,
s'io trovi un bacio che non ho dato!
35 Nel mio cantuccio d'ombra romita
lascia ch'io pianga su la mia vita!

E suona ancora l'ora, e mi squilla
due volte un grido quasi di cruccio,
e poi, tornata blanda e tranquilla,
40 mi persuade nel mio cantuccio:
è tardi! è l'ora! Sí, ritorniamo
dove son quelli ch'amano ed amo.

62 La mia sera

Il giorno fu pieno di lampi;
ma ora verranno le stelle,

le tacite stelle. Nei campi
c'è un breve *gre gre* di ranelle.
5   Le tremule foglie dei pioppi
trascorre una gioia leggiera.
Nel giorno, che lampi! che scoppi!
    Che pace, la sera!

Si devono aprire le stelle
10 nel cielo sí tenero e vivo.
Là, presso le allegre ranelle,
singhiozza monotono un rivo.
Di tutto quel cupo tumulto,
di tutta quell'aspra bufera,
15 non resta che un dolce singulto
    nell'umida sera.

È, quella infinita tempesta,
finita in un rivo canoro.
Dei fulmini fragili restano
20   cirri di porpora e d'oro.
O stanco dolore, riposa!
La nube nel giorno piú nera
fu quella che vedo piú rosa
    nell'ultima sera.

25 Che voli di rondini intorno!
che gridi nell'aria serena!
La fame del povero giorno
prolunga la garrula cena.
La parte, sí piccola, i nidi
30 nel giorno non l'ebbero intera.
Né io ... e che voli, che gridi,
    mia limpida sera!

Don ... Don ... E mi dicono, Dormi!
mi cantano, Dormi! sussurrano,
35   Dormi! bisbigliano, Dormi!

là, voci di tenebra azzurra . . .
Mi sembrano canti di culla,
che fanno ch'io torni com'era . . .
sentivo mia madre . . . poi nulla . . .
40   sul far della sera.

63   La servetta di monte

Sono usciti tutti. La serva
è in cucina, sola e selvaggia.
In un canto siede ed osserva
tanti rami appesi alla staggia.
5 Fa un giro con gli occhi, e bel bello
ritorna a guardarsi il pannello.

Non c'è nulla ch'essa conosca.
Tutto pende tacito e tetro.
E non ode che qualche mosca
10 che d'un tratto ronza ad un vetro;
non ode che il croccolío roco
che rende la pentola al fuoco.

Il musino aguzzo del topo
è apparito ad uno spiraglio.
15 È sparito, per venir dopo:
fa già l'acqua qualche sonaglio . . .
Lontano lontano lontano
si sente sonare un campano.

È un muletto per il sentiero,
20 che s'arrampica su su su;
che tra i faggi piccolo e nero
si vede e non si vede piú.
Ma il suo campanaccio si sente
sonare continuamente.

25 È forse anco un'ora di giorno.
C'è nell'aria un fiocco di luna.
Come è dolce questo ritorno
nella sera che non imbruna!
per una di queste serate!
30 tra tanto odorino d'estate!

La ragazza guarda, e non sente
piú il campano che a quando a quando.
Glielo vela forse il torrente
che a' suoi piedi cade scrosciando;
35 se forse non glielo nasconde
la brezza che scuote le fronde;

od il canto dell'usignolo
che, tacendo passero e cincia,
solo solo con l'assïuolo
40 la sua lunga veglia comincia,
ch'ha fine su l'alba, alla squilla,
nel cielo, della tottavilla.

64 La cavalla storna

Nella Torre il silenzio era già alto.
Sussurravano i pioppi del Rio Salto.

I cavalli normanni alle lor poste
frangean la biada con rumor di croste.

5 Là in fondo la cavalla era, selvaggia,
nata tra i pini su la salsa spiaggia;

che nelle froge avea del mar gli spruzzi
ancora, e gli urli negli orecchi aguzzi.

Con su la greppia un gomito, da essa
10 era mia madre; e le dicea sommessa:

«O cavallina, cavallina storna,
che portavi colui che non ritorna;

tu capivi il suo cenno ed il suo detto!
Egli ha lasciato un figlio giovinetto;

15 il primo d'otto tra miei figli e figlie;
e la sua mano non toccò mai briglie.

Tu che ti senti ai fianchi l'uragano,
tu dài retta alla sua piccola mano.

Tu ch'hai nel cuore la marina brulla,
20 tu dài retta alla sua voce fanciulla».

La cavalla volgea la scarna testa
verso mia madre, che dicea piú mesta:

«O cavallina, cavallina storna,
che portavi colui che non ritorna;

25 lo so, lo so, che tu l'amavi forte!
Con lui c'eri tu sola e la sua morte.

O nata in selve tra l'ondate e il vento,
tu tenesti nel cuore il tuo spavento;

sentendo lasso nella bocca il morso,
30 nel cuor veloce tu premesti il corso:

adagio seguitasti la tua via,
perché facesse in pace l'agonia . . .»

La scarna lunga testa era daccanto
al dolce viso di mia madre in pianto.

35 «O cavallina, cavallina storna,
che portavi colui che non ritorna;

oh! due parole egli dové pur dire!
E tu capisci, ma non sai ridire.

Tu con le briglie sciolte tra le zampe,
40 con dentro gli occhi il fuoco delle vampe,

con negli orecchi l'eco degli scoppi,
seguitasti la via tra gli alti pioppi:

lo riportavi tra il morir del sole,
perché udissimo noi le sue parole».

45 Stava attenta la lunga testa fiera.
Mia madre l'abbracciò su la criniera

«O cavallina, cavallina storna,
portavi a casa sua chi non ritorna!

a me, chi non ritornerà piú mai!
50 Tu fosti buona... Ma parlar non sai!

Tu non sai, poverina; altri non osa.
Oh! ma tu devi dirmi una una cosa!

Tu l'hai veduto l'uomo che l'uccise:
esso t'è qui nelle pupille fise.

55 Chi fu? Chi è? Ti voglio dire un nome.
E tu fa cenno. Dio t'insegni, come».

Ora, i cavalli non frangean la biada:
dormian sognando il bianco della strada.

La paglia non battean con l'unghie vuote:
60 dormian sognando il rullo delle ruote.

Mia madre alzò nel gran silenzio un dito:
disse un nome... Sonò alto un nitrito.

65 La tessitrice

Mi son seduto su la panchetta
come una volta... quanti anni fa?

Ella, come una volta, s'è stretta
su la panchetta.

5 E non il suono d'una parola;
solo un sorriso tutto pietà.
La bianca mano lascia la spola.

Piango, e le dico: Come ho potuto,
dolce mio bene, partir da te?
10 Piange, e mi dice d'un cenno muto:
Come hai potuto?

Con un sospiro quindi la cassa
tira del muto pettine a sé.
Muta la spola passa e ripassa.

15 Piango, e le chiedo: Perché non suona
dunque l'arguto pettine piú?
Ella mi fissa timida e buona:
Perché non suona?

E piange, e piange — Mio dolce amore,
20 non t'hanno detto? non lo sai tu?
Io non son viva che nel tuo cuore.

Morta! Sí, morta! Se tesso, tesso
per te soltanto; come, non so;
in questa tela, sotto il cipresso,
25 accanto alfine ti dormirò. —

POEMI CONVIVIALI

66 Solon

Triste il convito senza canto, come
tempio senza votivo oro di doni;
ché questo è bello: attendere al cantore
che nella voce ha l'eco dell'Ignoto.
5 Oh! nulla, io dico, è bello piú, che udire
un buon cantore, placidi, seduti
l'un presso l'altro, avanti mense piene
di pani biondi e di fumanti carni,
mentre il fanciullo dal cratere attinge
10 vino, e lo porta e versa nelle coppe;
e dire in tanto grazïosi detti,
mentre la cetra inalza il suo sacro inno;
o dell'auleta querulo, che piange,
godere, poi che ti si muta in cuore
15 il suo dolore in tua felicità.

«Solon, dicesti un giorno tu: Beato
chi ama, chi cavalli ha solidunghi,
cani da preda, un ospite lontano.
Ora te né lontano ospite giova
20 né, già vecchio, i bei cani né cavalli
di solid'unghia, né l'amore, o savio.
Te la coppa ora giova: ora tu lodi
piú vecchio il vino e piú novello il canto.
E novelle al Pireo, con la bonaccia
25 prima e co' primi stormi, due canzoni
oltremarine giunsero. Le reca
una donna d'Eresso». «Apri:» rispose;
«alla rondine, o Phoco, apri la porta».

Erano le Anthesterïe: s'apriva
30 il fumeo doglio e si saggiava il vino.

   Entrò, col lume della primavera
   e con l'alito salso dell'Egeo,
   la cantatrice. Ella sapea due canti:
   l'uno, d'amore, l'altro era di morte.
35 Entrò pensosa; e Phoco le porgeva
   uno sgabello d'auree borchie ornato
   ed una coppa. Ella sedé, reggendo
   la risonante pèctide; ne strinse
   tacita intorno ai còllabi le corde;
40 tentò le corde fremebonde, e disse:

   Splende al plenilunïo l'orto; il melo
   trema appena d'un tremolio d'argento...
   Nei lontani monti color di cielo
           sibila il vento.

45 Mugghia il vento, strepita tra le forre,
   su le quercie gettasi... Il mio non sembra
   che un tremore, ma è l'amore, e corre,
           spossa le membra!

   M'è lontano dalle ricciute chiome,
50 quanto il sole; sí, ma mi giunge al cuore,
   come il sole: bello, ma bello come
           sole che muore.

   Dileguare! e altro non voglio: voglio
   farmi chiarità che da lui si effonda.
55 Scoglio estremo della gran luce, scoglio
           su la grande onda,

   dolce è da te scendere dove è pace:
   scende il sole nell'infinito mare;
   trema e scende la chiarità seguace
60   crepuscolare.

«La Morte è questa!» il vecchio esclamò. «Questo,»
ella rispose, «è, ospite, l'Amore».
Tentò le corde fremebonde, e disse:

Togli il pianto. È colpa! Sei del poeta
65   nella casa, tu. Chi dirà che fui?
Piangi il morto atleta: beltà d'atleta
        muore con lui.

Muore la virtú dell'eroe che il cocchio
spinge urlando tra le nemiche schiere;
70   muore il seno, sí, di Rhodòpi, l'occhio
        del timoniere;

ma non muore il canto che tra il tintinno
della pèctide apre il candor dell'ale.
E il poeta fin che non muoia l'inno,
75   vive, immortale,

poi che l'inno (diano le rosee dita
pace al peplo, a noi non s'addice il lutto)
è la nostra forza e beltà, la vita,
        l'anima, tutto!

80   E chi voglia me rivedere, tocchi
queste corde, canti un mio canto: in quella,
tutta rose rimireranno gli occhi
        Saffo la bella.

Questo era il canto della Morte; e il vecchio
85   Solon qui disse: «Ch'io l'impari, e muoia».

67 Il sonno di Odisseo

I

Per nove giorni, e notte e dí, la nave
nera filò, ché la portava il vento

e il timoniere, e ne reggeva accorta
la grande mano d'Odisseo le scotte;
5 né, lasso, ad altri le cedea, ché verso
la cara patria lo portava il vento.
Per nove giorni, e notte e dí, la nera
nave filò, né l'occhio mai distolse
l'eroe, cercando l'isola rupestre
10 tra il cilestrino tremolío del mare;
pago se prima di morir vedesse
balzarne in aria i vortici del fumo.
Nel decimo, là dove era vanito
il nono sole in un barbaglio d'oro,
15 ora gli apparse non sapea che nero:
nuvola o terra? E gli balenò vinto
dall'alba dolce il grave occhio: e lontano
s'immerse il cuore d'Odisseo nel sonno.

II

E venne incontro al volo della nave,
20 ecco, una terra, e veleggiava azzurra
tra il cilestrino tremolío del mare;
e con un monte ella prendea del cielo,
e giú dal monte spumeggiando i botri
scendean tra i ciuffi dell'irsute stipe;
25 e ne' suoi poggi apparvero i filari
lunghi di viti, ed a' suoi piedi i campi
vellosi della nuova erba del grano:
e tutta apparve un'isola rupestre,
dura, non buona a pascere polledri,
30 ma sí di capre e sí di buoi nutrice:
e qua e là sopra gli aerei picchi
morian nel chiaro dell'aurora i fuochi
de' mandrïani; e qua e là sbalzava
il mattutino vortice del fumo,
35 d'Itaca, alfine: ma non già lo vide
notando il cuore d'Odisseo nel sonno.

III

    Ed ecco a prua dell'incavata nave
volar parole, simili ad uccelli,
con fuggevoli sibili. La nave
40 radeva allora il picco alto del Corvo
e il ben cerchiato fonte; e se n'udiva
un grufolare fragile di verri;
ed ampio un chiuso si scorgea, di grandi
massi ricinto ed assiepato intorno
45 di salvatico pero e di prunalbo;
ed il divino mandrïan dei verri,
presso la spiaggia, della nera scorza
spogliava con l'aguzza ascia un querciolo,
e grandi pali a rinforzare il chiuso
50 poi ne tagliò coi morsi aspri dell'ascia;
e sí e no tra lo sciacquío dell'onde
giungeva al mare il roco ansar dei colpi,
d'Eumeo fedele: ma non già li udiva
tuffato il cuore d'Odisseo nel sonno.

IV

55   E già da prua, sopra la nave, a poppa,
simili a freccie, andavano parole
con fuggevoli fremiti. La nave
era di faccia al porto di Forkyne;
e in capo ad esso si vedea l'olivo,
60 grande, fronzuto, e presso quello un antro:
l'antro d'affaccendate api sonoro,
quando in crateri ed anfore di pietra
filano la soave opra del miele:
e si scorgeva la sassosa strada
65 della città: si distinguea, tra il verde
d'acquosi ontani, la fontana bianca
e l'ara bianca, ed una eccelsa casa:
l'eccelsa casa d'Odisseo: già forse

stridea la spola fra la trama, e sotto
70 le stanche dita ricrescea la tela,
ampia, immortale... Oh! non udí né vide
perduto il cuore d'Odisseo nel sonno.

V

E su la nave, nell'entrare il porto,
il peggio vinse: sciolsero i compagni
75 gli otri, e la furia ne fischiò dei venti:
la vela si svoltò, si sbatté, come
peplo, cui donna abbandonò disteso
ad inasprire sopra aereo picco:
ecco, e la nave lontanò dal porto;
80 e un giovinetto stava già nel porto,
poggiato all'asta dalla bronzea punta:
e il giovinetto sotto il glauco olivo
stava pensoso; ed un veloce cane
correva intorno a lui scodinzolando:
85 e il cane dalle volte irrequïete
sostò, con gli occhi all'infinito mare;
e com'ebbe le salse orme fiutate,
ululò dietro la fuggente nave:
Argo, il suo cane: ma non già l'udiva
90 tuffato il cuore d'Odisseo nel sonno.

VI

E la nave radeva ora una punta
d'Itaca scabra. E tra due poggi un campo
era, ben culto; il campo di Laerte;
del vecchio re; col fertile pometo;
95 coi peri e meli che Laerte aveva
donati al figlio tuttavia fanciullo;
ché lo seguiva per la vigna, e questo
chiedeva degli snelli albèri e quello:
tredici peri e dieci meli in fila

100 stavano, bianchi della lor fiorita:
all'ombra d'uno, all'ombra del piú bianco,
era un vecchio, poggiato su la marra:
il vecchio, volto all'infinito mare
dove mugghiava il subito tumulto,
105 limando ai faticati occhi la luce,
riguardò dietro la fuggente nave:
era suo padre: ma non già lo vide
notando il cuore d'Odisseo nel sonno.

VII

Ed i venti portarono la nave
110 nera piú lungi. E subito aprí gli occhi
l'eroe, rapidi aprí gli occhi a vedere
sbalzar dalla sognata Itaca il fumo;
e scoprir forse il fido Eumeo nel chiuso
ben cinto, e forse il padre suo nel campo
115 ben culto: il padre che sopra la marra
appoggiato guardasse la sua nave;
e forse il figlio che poggiato all'asta
la sua nave guardasse: e lo seguiva,
certo, e intorno correa scodinzolando
120 Argo, il suo cane; e forse la sua casa,
la dolce casa ove la fida moglie
già percorreva il garrulo telaio:
guardò: ma vide non sapea che nero
fuggire per il violaceo mare,
125 nuvola o terra? e dileguar lontano,
emerso il cuore d'Odisseo dal sonno.

POEMI ITALICI

68 Paulo Ucello

CAP. I

IN PRIMA COME PAULO DIPINTORE FIORENTINO S'INVOGLIÒ
D'UN MONACHINO O CIUFFOLOTTO E NON POTÉ COMPRARLO
E ALLORA LO DIPINSE

Di buona ora tornato all'abituro
Paulo di Dono non finí un mazzocchio
ch'egli scortava. Dipingea sul muro

un monachino che tenea nell'occhio
5   dalla mattina, che con Donatello
e ser Filippo era ristato a crocchio.

Quelli compravan uova. Esso un fringuello
in gabbia vide, dietro il banco, rosso
cinabro il petto, e nero un suo mantello;

10   nero un cappuccio ed un mantello indosso.
Paulo di Dono era assai trito e parco;
ma lo comprava, se ci aveva un grosso.

Ma non l'aveva. Andò a dipinger l'arco
di porta a San Tomaso. E gli avveniva
15   di dire: È un fraticino di San Marco.

Ne tornò presto. Era una sera estiva
piena di voli. Il vecchio quella sera
dimenticò la dolce prospettiva.

Dipingea con la sua bella maniera
20   nella parete, al fiammeggiar del cielo.

E il monachino rosso, ecco, lí era,

posato sopra un ramuscel di melo.

CAP. II

DELLA PARETE CHE PAULO DIPINGEVA NELLA STANZUOLA, PER SUA GIOIA, CON ALBERI E CAMPI IN PROSPETTIVA

Ché la parete verzicava tutta
d'alberi: pini dalle ombrelle nere
25 e fichi e meli; ed erbe e fiori e frutta.

E sí, meraviglioso era a vedere
che biancheggiava il mandorlo di fiori,
e gialle al pero già pendean le pere.

Lustravano nel sole alti gli allori:
30 sur una bruna bruna acqua di polle
l'edera andava con le foglie a cuori.

Sorgeva in fondo a grado a grado un colle,
o gremito di rosse uve sui tralci
o nereggiante d'ancor fresche zolle.

35 Lenti lungo il ruscello erano i salci,
lunghi per la sassosa erta i cipressi.
Qua zappe in terra si vedean, là falci.

E qua tra siepi quadre erano impressi
diritti solchi nel terren già rotto,
40 e là fiottava un biondo mar di messi.

E là, stupore, due bovi che sotto
il giogo aprivan grandi grandi un solco,
non eran grandi come era un leprotto

qua, che fuggiva a un urlo del bifolco.

CAP. III

COME IN ESSA PARETE AVEA DIPINTI D'OGNI SORTA UCCELLI, PER DILETTARSI IN VEDERLI, POI CHE AVERLI NON POTEVA

45 E uccelli, uccelli, uccelli, che il buon uomo
via via vedeva, e non potea comprare:
per terra, in acqua, presso un fiore o un pomo:

col ciuffo, con la cresta, col collare:
uccelli usi alla macchia, usi alla valle:
50 scesi dal monte, reduci dal mare:

con l'ali azzurre, rosse, verdi, gialle:
di neve, fuoco, terra, aria, le piume:
con entro il becco pippoli o farfalle.

Stormi di gru fuggivano le brume,
55 schiere di cigni come bianche navi
fendeano l'acqua d'un ceruleo fiume.

Veniano sparse alle lor note travi
le rondini. E tu, bruna aquila, a piombo
dal cielo in vano sopra lor calavi.

60 Ella era lí, pur cosí lungi! E il rombo
del suo gran volo, non l'udian le quaglie,
non l'udiva la tortore e il colombo.

Sicuri sulle stipe di sodaglie,
tranquilli su' falaschi di paduli,
65 stavano rosignoli, forapaglie,

cincie, verle, luí, fife, cuculi.

CAP. IV

COME MIRANDO LE CREATURE DEL SUO PENNELLO NON DISSE L'ANGELUS E FU TENTATO

Poi che senza né vischio ebbe né rete
anche, nella stanzuola, il ciuffolotto,

Paulo mirò la bella sua parete.

70 E non udí che gli avea fatto motto
la vecchia moglie; e non udí sonare
l'Avemaria dal campanil di Giotto.

Le creature sue piccole e care
mirava il terzïarïo canuto
75 nella serenità crepuscolare.

E non disse, com'era uso, il saluto
dell'angelo. Saliva alla finestra
un suono di vivuola e di leuto.

Chiara la sera, l'aria era silvestra:
80 regamo e persa uliva sui balconi,
e giuncava le vie fior di ginestra.

Passeri arguti empían gli archi e gli sproni
incominciati di ser Brunellesco.
Cantavano laggiú donne e garzoni.

85 C'era tanto sussurro e tanto fresco
intorno a te, Santa Maria del fiore!
E Paulo si scordò Santo Francesco,

e fu tentato, e mormorò nel cuore.

CAP. V

DELLA MORMORAZIONE CHE FECE PAULO, IL QUALE
AVREBBE PUR VOLUTO ALCUN UCCELLINO VIVO

Pensava: «Io sono delle pecorelle,
90 Madonna Povertà, di tua pastura.
E qui non ha né fanti né fancelle.

E vivo di pan d'orzo e d'acqua pura.
E vo come la chiocciola ch'ha solo
quello ch'ha seco, a schiccherar le mura.

95 Oh! non voglio un podere in Cafaggiolo,
come Donato: ma un cantuccio d'orto
sí, con un pero, un melo, un azzeruolo.

Ch'egli è pur, credo, il singolar conforto
un capodaglio per chi l'ha piantato!
100 Basta. Di bene, io ho questo in iscorto,

dipinto a secco. E s'io non son Donato,
son primo in far paesi, alberi, e sono
pur da quanto chi vende uova in mercato.

Ora, al nome di Dio, Paulo di Dono
105 sta contento, poderi, orti, a vederli:
ma un rosignolo io lo vorrei di buono.

Uno di questi picchi o questi merli,
in casa, che ci sia, non che ci paia!
un uccellino vero, uno che sverli,

110 e mi consoli nella mia vecchiaia».

CAP. VI

COME SANTO FRANCESCO DISCESE PER LA BELLA
PROSPETTIVA CHE PAULO AVEVA DIPINTA, E LO RIMBROTTÒ

Cotale fu la mormorazione,
sommessa, in cuore. Ma dagli alti cieli
l'intese il fi di Pietro Bernardone.

Ecco e dal colle tra le viti e i meli
115 Santo Francesco discendea bel bello
sull'erba senza ripiegar gli steli.

Era scalzo, e vestito di bigello.
E di lunge, venendo a fronte a fronte,
diceva: «O frate Paulo cattivello!

120 Dunque tu non vuoi piú che, presso un fonte,
del tuo pezzuol di pane ora ti pasca

la Povertà che sta con Dio sul monte!

Non vuoi piú, frate Paulo, ciò che casca
dalla mensa degli angeli, e vorresti
125 danaro e verga e calzamenti e tasca!

O Paulo uccello, sii come i foresti
fratelli tuoi! Ché chi non ha, non pecca.
Non disïare argento, oro, due vesti.

Buona è codesta, color foglia secca,
130 tale qual ha la tua sirocchia santa,
la lodoletta, che ben sai che becca

due grani in terra, e vola in cielo, e canta».

CAP. VII

COME IL SANTO INTESE CHE IL DESÍO DI PAULO ERA DI POCO ED EI GLI MOSTRÒ CHE ERA DI TANTO

Cosí dicendo egli aggrandía pian piano,
e gli fu presso, e con un gesto pio
135 gli pose al petto sopra il cuor la mano.

Non vi sentí se non un tremolío,
d'ale d'uccello. Onde riprese il Santo:
«O frate Paulo, poverel di Dio!

È poco a te quel che desii, ma tanto
140 per l'uccellino che tu vuoi prigione
perché gioia a te faccia del suo pianto!

E' bramerebbe sempre il suo Mugnone
o il suo Galluzzo, in cui vivea mendico
dando per ogni bruco una canzone.

145 O frate Paulo, in verità ti dico
che meglio al bosco un vermicciòl gli aggrada
che in gabbia un alberello di panico.

Lasciali andare per la loro strada
cantando laudi, il bel mese di maggio,
150 odorati di sole e di rugiada!

A' miei frati minori il mio retaggio
lascia! la dolce vita solitaria,
i monti, la celluzza sur un faggio,

il chiostro con la gran cupola d'aria!»

CAP. VIII

COME IL SANTO PARTENDOSI DA PAULO, CHE PUR BRAMAVA
SÍ PICCOLA COSA, DISSE A LUI UNA GRANDE PAROLA

155 Partiva, rialzando ora il cappuccio:
ché con l'ignuda Povertà tranquilla
Paulo avea pace dopo il breve cruccio.

Lasciava Paulo, al suono d'una squilla
lontana, quando quel tremolío d'ale
160 d'uccello vide nella sua pupilla.

Ne lagrimò, ché ben sapea che male
non era in quel desío povero e vano,
ch'unico aveva il fratel suo mortale.

Venía quel suono fievole e lontano
165 di squilla, lí dai monti, da un convento
che Paulo vi avea messo di sua mano.

Veniva il suono or sí or no col vento,
dai monti azzurri, per le valli cave;
e cullava il paese sonnolento.

170 Santo Francesco sussurrò: «Di' Ave
Maria»; poi senza ripiegar gli steli
movea sull'erba, e pur dicea soave:

«Sei come uccello ch'uomini crudeli
hanno accecato, o dolce frate uccello!

175 E cerchi il sole, e ne son pieni i cieli,

e cerchi un chicco, e pieno è l'alberello».

CAP. IX

COME IL SANTO GLI MOSTRÒ CHE GLI UCCELLI CHE PAULO
AVEVA DIPINTI, ERANO VERI E VIVI ANCH'ESSI, E SUOI
SOL ESSI

E lontanando si gettava avanti,
a mo' di pio seminator, le brice
cadute al vostro desco, angeli santi.

180 Paulo guardava, timido, in tralice.
Le miche egli attingeva dallo scollo
del cappuccio, e spargea per la pendice.

Ecco avveniva un murmure, uno sgrollo
di foglie, come a un soffio di libeccio.
185 Scattò il colombo mollemente il collo.

Si levava un sommesso cicaleccio,
fin che sonò la dolce voce mesta
delle fedeli tortole del Greccio.

Dal campo, dal verzier, dalla foresta
190 scesero a lui gli uccelli, ai piedi, ai fianchi,
in grembo, sulle braccia, sulla testa.

Vennero a lui le quaglie coi lor branchi
di piccolini, a lui vennero a schiera
sull'acque azzurre i grandi cigni bianchi.

195 E sminuiva, e già di lui non c'era,
sui monti, che cinque stelline d'oro.
E, come bruscinar di primavera,

rimase un trito becchettío sonoro.

CAP. X

ALL'ULTIMO COME CANTÒ IL ROSIGNOLO, E PAULO ERA ADDORMITO

    E poi sparí. Poi, come fu sparito,
200 l'usignolo cantò da un arbuscello,
    e chiese dov'era ito ... ito ... ito ...

    Ne stormí con le foglie dell'ornello,
    ne sibilò coi gambi del frumento,
    ne gorgogliò con l'acqua del ruscello.

205 E tacque un poco, e poi sommesso e lento
    ne interrogò le nubi a una a una;
    poi con un trillo alto ne chiese al vento.

    E poi ne pianse al lume della luna,
    bianca sul greto, tremula sul prato;
210 che alluminava nella stanza bruna

    il vecchio dipintore addormentato.

ODI E INNI

69   A una morta

O tu che sei tra i vivi
solo perché ti penso;
come se odor d'incenso
    fosse il pino che fu;

5   ma con me vivi, vivi
tu pure un po': tremando
l'attimo io vedo, quando
    non ti penserò piú!

Resta di me, pensiero!
10   Ch'io creda, o Dio! Tuoi servi,
Morte, sian vene e nervi;
    pensiero, anima, no!

Ch'io resti col pensiero,
che non si estingua mai!
15   E sempre in me sarai,
    in te sempre sarò.

Ma . . . Oh! l'eterna doglia
del mio pensiero sperso,
quando nell'Universo
20   cerchi ciò che non v'è!

quando le braccia voglia
per ricondurti al seno!
la bocca! gli occhi! almeno
    perch'io pianga su te!

70 Il cane notturno

Nell'alta notte sento tra i queruli
trilli di grilli, sento tra il murmure
    piovoso del Serchio che in piena
    trascorre nell'ombra serena,

5 là nell'oscura valle dov'errano
sole, da niuno viste, le lucciole,
    sonare da fratte lontane
    velato il latrato d'un cane.

Chi là, passando tardo per tacite
10 strade, fra nere siepi di bussolo,
    con l'eco dei passi, in un'aia
    destava quel cane, che abbaia?

Parte? ritorna? Lagrima? dubita?
ha in cuor parole chiuse che battono
15   col suono d'alterno oriuolo?
    ha un'ombra, ch'è sola con solo?

Va! Va! gli dice la voce vigile
sonando irosa di tra le tenebre.
    Traspare dagli alberi folti
20   la casa, che sembra che ascolti . . .

come tra il sonno, chiuse le palpebre
sue grandi . . . L'uomo dorme, ed un memore
    suo braccio, sul letto di foglie,
    sta presso la florida moglie.

25 E dorme nella zana di vetrici
la bimba, e gli altri piccoli dormono.
    S'inseguono al buio con ali
    di mosche i lor aliti uguali.

Uguali uguali, passano tornano

30 con ronzío lieve, dentro le tenebre
      cercandosi: e l'anime ancora,
      si cercano, sino all'aurora,

    per le ignorate lunghe viottole
    del sonno; e al fine si ricongiungono;
35   e scoppia sul fare del giorno
      l'allegro vocío del ritorno.

71 L'isola dei poeti

Il treno andava. Gli occhi a me la brezza
pungea tra quella ignota ombra lontana;
e m'invadea le vene la dolcezza
      antelucana:

5 e il capo mi si abbandonò. Tra i crolli
del treno allora non udii che un frùscio
uguale: il sonno avea spinto sui molli
      cardini l'uscio,

e, di là d'esso, il fragor ferreo parve
10 piano e lontano. Ed ecco udii, ricordo,
il metro uguale, tra un vocío di larve,
      del tetracordo:

di là dal sonno, alcuno udii narrare
le due Sirene e il loro incantamento,
15 e la lor voce aerea, di mare
      fatta e di vento:

gli udii narrare l'isola del Sole,
là dove mandre e greggie solitarie
pascono, e vanno dietro lor due sole
20   grandi armentarie,

con grandi pepli . . . Ed il tinnir cedeva

ad un'arguta melodia di canne:
udii cantare il fumo che si leva
        dalle capanne,

25 le siepi in fiore, i mezzodí d'estate
pieni d'un verso inerte di cicale,
e rombi delle cupe arnie, e ventate
        fresche di sale:

e chi cantava forse era un pastore
30 tutto nascosto tra le verdi fronde:
chiaro latrava un cane tra il fragore
        vasto dell'onde.

Ecco e le cetre levano il tintinno
dorico, misto allo squillar del loto
35 chiarosonante. Ed improvviso un inno
        sbalza nel vuoto:

l'aquila è in alto: fulgida nel lume
del sole: preda ha negli artigli: lente
ondeggiando cadono giú piume
40   sanguinolente:

in alto in alto, sopra i gioghi bianchi
d'Etna, piú su de' piccoli occhi torvi:
nelle bassure crocitano branchi
        neri di corvi.

45 Quel crocitare mi destò. Di fronte
m'eri, o Sicilia, o nuvola di rosa
sorta dal mare! E nell'azzurro un monte:
        l'Etna nevosa.

Salve, o Sicilia! Ogni aura che qui muove,
50 pulsa una cetra od empie una zampogna,
e canta e passa ... Io era giunto dove
        giunge chi sogna;

chi sogna, ed apre bianche vele ai venti
nel tempo oscuro, in dubbio se all'aurora
55 l'ospite lui ravvisi, dopo venti
        secoli, ancora.

72   Inno degli emigrati italiani a Dante

Esule a cui ciascuno fu crudele;
tu cui da sé la dolce patria scisse
e spinse in mare legno senza vele . . .

Ma tu scendesti a interrogare Ulisse
5 il molto errante, il molto paziënte,
e ci dicesti ciò ch'egli ti disse:

— Uomini, non credete all'occidente:
ciò ch'è a voi sera è prima aurora altrui.
Seguite me nel mondo senza gente:
10 dire, anche morti, gioverà: Vi fui! —

Profeta, e tu, lungo l'Oceano insonne
dicevi ad uno insonne sulle porte
schiuse e vietate: — Non ci son colonne!

Le pose a segno Ercole eroe, che in sorte
15 ebbe l'eterna Gioventú ribelle.
Le pose il forte: passa oltre il piú forte.

Va! Salpa! Issa le vele! Cerca stelle
piú nuove, ignoti mari e vie sul rombo
di venti ignoti, e le tre caravelle
20 ad altre terre adduci ormai, Colombo. —

O timonier d'Italia eterno, Dante!
Sei tu che volgi dove vuoi la prora
sul nostro lungo solco spumeggiante!

Con lui tu fosti: governavi allora

25 *Santa Maria*, quando sul limitare
del nuovo Mondo, ella attendea l'aurora.

Prima dell'alba, sul purpureo mare
quasi una grigia nuvola apparí...
«Terra!» gridò la *Pinta*, ed echeggiare
30 parve una voce alta infinita: — Sí!

Castelvecchio, 1911.

NOTES AND VOCABULARY

ABBREVIATIONS
USED IN THE NOTES AND VOCABULARY

adj.	adjective	m.	masculine
adv.	adverb	met.	metaphorical
arch.	archaic	n.	noun
cf.	compare	naut.	nautical
f.	feminine	poet.	poetic
f, ff	and the following line(s)	p.p.	past participle
		pl.	plural
fig.	figurative(ly)	prep.	preposition
gen.	genitive	pron.	pronoun
impers.	impersonal	rfl.	reflexive
indef.	indefinite	sing.	singular
inf.	infinitive	subj.	subject
intrans.	intransitive	trans.	transitive
invar.	invariable		

NOTES

The date assigned to a poem refers to the year in which it was first published in its final form.

MYRICAE

The title, which is an allusion to the *humiles ... myricae* of the second line of Virgil's fourth eclogue, designates not inappropriately the type of composition (brief, low-keyed, of limited compass, on a commonplace subject) in which the collection abounds. Many poems are descriptive — of nature, domestic interiors, the poet's own family circle, aspects of the countryside and country life in Romagna and the Tuscan Maremma — but there are also nostalgic reminiscences, reflections on life and poetry, and gloomy commemorations of tragic events in the history of the Pascoli family. The mood varies from the idyllic and carefree to the gloomy and embittered, with moments of dark depression. The later poems tend to be more sombre in mood than the earlier ones, and some of them have symbolic meanings which the earlier ones lack.

1. *Alba festiva* (1894)

The poem captures the sound of church-bells, whose clamour fills the calm air of dawn. The sombre close (lines 16-9) contrasts with the conversational, almost casual tone of the opening lines and the prevailing mood of cheerful serenity to which the title alludes. In respect of technique the poem has been aptly likened to Poe's *The Bells*. *Settenari* in *terza rima*.

1 **Che hanno** conversational idiom. Cf. *Che hai*? ('What's the matter with you?').

2f **squillano ... ronzano** Pascoli's use of sound-contrasts in this poem is discussed in the Introduction.

8 **implori** normally a transitive verb; here used absolutely, i.e. without an object. See also *adoro* in lines 12f.

12–14 The punctuation indicates two pieces of direct

speech: the smaller bells urge the deeper ones to sound again their note of adoration.

13 **Dilla** = *Di'* (imperative of *dire*) + *la* (object pronoun anticipating *la nota d'oro*).

14 **L'onda** the wave of sound that appears to 'hang' in the air. Note the bold metaphor.

17f **amor ... desío** The religious overtones (love of God, longing for paradise) reinforce earlier suggestions that the bells are engaged in an act of worship: *inno, implori, cantico, adoro*.

18 **par** = *pare* impersonal use.

2. *Speranze e memorie* (1896)

Antithetical images (white against a dark background, black against a light background) suggest the opposite states of mind occasioned first by the poet's hopes, then by his memories. Alternating *ottonari* and *quaternari* with the rhyme scheme AbAbXa, the verses being linked by the common ending X (*sogni*).

1 **Paranzelle** object of *vedeva*.
in alto mare 'out at sea'.

3 **io vedeva** The ending in *-a* of the 1st person singular of the imperfect indicative was normal in Pascoli's time.
palpitare 'quiver', referring (like the adjective *bianche*) to the sails of the boat.

4 **come** 'as though'.

6 **per** literally 'all over'; also in line 12.

7–9 **credo in cielo/rivedere** Pascoli alludes to the common visual experience of after-sensations produced in the retina of the eye after exposure to a strong light stimulus. Black and white are reversed as in a photographic negative.

9 **velo** a black mourning veil.

3. *Allora* (1897)

A poem about the transient nature of happiness. *Novenari* in quatrains with alternate rhyme.

1 **lunge** = *lungi*, literally 'far off'; here 'long ago', 'in the distant past'.

5 **per** 'throughout'.

12 **sí ... sí** 'both ... and'.

14 **in vero** = *infatti*.

15f   Construe: *ma così bello, quel punto, che ero molto felice, felice.*

4. *Patria* (1894)

Day-dreaming, the poet imagines he is in his native Romagna until the angelus-bell awakens him to reality. The situation, ambiguous at the outset, becomes clear only in the penultimate line. *Settenari* organized in a form reminiscent of the old Italian *ballata* with the scheme X ABABX CDCDX. In the first half of the poem lines are linked by assonance as well as by rhyme: *-are, -ale, -ate; -ole, -ose.*

Patria   The word is used of one's native country, district, town or village. It is the place of one's birth. Here the emotional associations of the word are similar to those of the English word 'home'.

1   **Sogno**   may be an intransitive verb (so 'I dream of') or a noun; if the latter, the meaning may be 'a dream *of* a summer's day' or 'a dream *on* a summer's day'; the ambiguity helps to confuse dream with waking reality.

2   **scampanellare**   'trilling'; the word (literally 'to ring a bell long and loud') is used figuratively.

4   **Stridule**   agrees with *foglie*, but has adverbial force.
pel filare (*per + il*) 'all along . . .'.

7   **Scendeä** = *Scendeva*   The word is to be pronounced as two syllables with syneresis between the vowels of the termination. Analogous forms are available for the third person plural (*-éano*) and for the corresponding endings of the imperfect indicative of verbs in *-ire* (*-ía, -íano*). They are common in poetry for reasons of metrical convenience, though modern prose usage requires the retention of the intervocalic *v*. In old Italian the two forms are found side by side in prose.

10   **róse:**   past participle of *rodere.*

5. *Il nunzio* (1897)

The harmless bumble-bee becomes, in the poet's imagination, a harbinger of death. He draws on a popular superstition that a bumble-bee in the house portends the arrival of news: good, if the insect is golden; bad, if the insect is black. Metre: similar to that of No. **4**, but single stanzas replace pairs of stanzas, and the poem is in *senari*. The impression of monotony in the movement is due to the even syllable-count and to the frequent use of lines that divide into equal halves.

   12 **morti** an allusion to members of the poet's family now dead.

6. *La cucitrice* (1896)

The impenetrable private world of the individual is suggested by a description of a woman sitting at her window sewing. *Ottonari* with alternate rhyme: ABABX; stanzas linked by their last lines, which rhyme together.

   1 **per** See note on *pel filare* (4.4).

   7 **covata** literally 'brood' (of chickens, etc.); here used figuratively of a group of children. (Some commentators read *covata* literally and take *maestra* in line 6 to mean *strada maestra*, 'main road').

7. *Romagna* (1897)

This nostalgic poem, in which Pascoli looks back to his boyhood in Romagna, is a reworking of a much earlier poem (*Epistola a Ridiverde*) started in 1878. As *Romagna* it appeared in a different version in 1892. It is addressed to Pascoli's friend Severino Ferrari (1856–1905), poet and teacher at Bologna University, who like the poet came from Romagna. *Endecasillabi* in quatrains with alternate rhyme.

   3 **paese** 'region'.

andando used absolutely, the unexpressed subject being different from that of the main verb *accompagna*: 'as one goes about'.

ci: The pronoun here corresponds to the English indefinite pronoun 'one'.

   4 **San Marino** The tiny independent republic of San Marino is situated on a hill that rises from the coastal plain about ten miles south of San Mauro.

   6 **cui** = *che* direct object of **regnarono** ('ruled'): two archaisms that betray the early date of the poem in its original version. Cf. notes on lines 20, 27.

Guidi e Malatesta powerful families with possessions in Romagna in the time of Dante; familiar names to readers of the *Divine Comedy*.

   7 **il Passator(e)** nickname (literally 'the Ferryman', an allusion to his occupation) of a famous bandit called Stefano

NOTES 139

Pelloni (1824–51), still a local folk-hero in Pascoli's day. His generosity was legendary, like that of Ghino di Tacco, the bandit-hero of Boccaccio's tale, *Decameron*, X.2.

cortese: 'generous'.

9 **singhiozzando** onomatopoeic.

11 **lustreggianti** = *lustri* 'glittering'.

12 **iridata** = *iridescente* 'iridescent'.

13–15 **perderci ... gettarci** exclamatory infinitives following the exclamation at the beginning of line 13. (Cf. 'Oh, to be in England ...').

14 **di tra** = *tra*.

nido alle g. 'nesting-place for ...'

18 **scodella** a bowl from which to eat.

19 **'l** = *il*.

opache = *oscure* 'dark'.

20 **laboriosa** The epithet is transferred from the act of chewing to the fodder itself: a trope with an old-fashioned sound.

21 **Da'** = *Dai*. Cf. line 28: *co'* = *coi*.

25 **bruciate** = *caldissime*.

26–8 **una mimosa** 'Era una mimosa arborescente, di cui non so il nome' (Pascoli). Most members of the Acacia family (known as 'mimosa' in Europe) have yellow flowers, but the Persian acacia or silk tree (*Albizzia julibrissin*) with its fluffy pink flower-heads fits Pascoli's description well. See line 28.

27 **fioria** See note on *scendea* (**4.**7). The transitive use of the verb (= 'to adorn with flowers') belongs to the literary tradition. Cf. line 24: *fiorito d'occhi*.

29 **per** See note on *pel filare* (**4.**4).

32 **a giorni** 'at times'.

33ff **dove ... io galoppava ... o mi vedea presente** ... i.e. he read Ariosto and the memoirs of Napoleon.

34f **Guidon Selvaggio ... Astolfo** two of the knights of Charlemagne in Ariosto's *Orlando furioso* and earlier chivalrous epics: Astolfo, the English knight; Guidone, nicknamed 'the Savage', half-brother to Rinaldo.

35 **mi vedea presente** *mi* is an indirect object pronoun: 'I could see before me'.

36 **l'imperatore** = Napoleon.

eremitaggio: an allusion to the isolation of the house where Napoleon lived during his exile on St Helena and where he dictated his memoirs.

37 **aereo** 'airborne'.

38 **l'ippogrifo** the hippogriff: the winged horse used by Astolfo as a means of aerial transport.

pel sognato alone At the literal level this is an allusion to Astolfo's journey to the Earthly Paradise and thence to the moon: *alone* = the halo or ring that is sometimes seen around the moon; *sognato*, like English 'dreamt of', has both literal and figurative (= 'eagerly desired') connotations.

41 **allor allor** 'just recently'. (Cf. *or ora* 'just now'.)

45 **quelli** *poemi* understood.

47 **frondi** plural of *fronde*, an old form of *fronda*, a leafy branch.

49—52 The stanza alludes to the dispersal of Pascoli's family and the premature death of so many of its members.

51 **patria** See note on the title of *Patria*.

55 **ch'io non ritrovi** 'so as not to discover'.

57—60 Cf. lines 5—8.

8. *Rio Salto* (1887)

The title refers to a brook which flowed near Pascoli's home at San Mauro. As in *Romagna* the object of the poet's nostalgia is not just the familiar landscape of his youth, but a whole world of youthful ideals and illusions. Sonnet.

1f **non era . . . palafreni** Construe: *'il suon che s'udìa nella valle fonda non era di palafreni'*.

4 **a furia** 'violently', 'furiously'.

5 **via e via per** 'on and on along'.

6 **cavalieri erranti** 'knights errant'.

8 **onda** poetic for 'water'.

13 **soave** adverb, 'softly'.

9. *I puffini dell'Adriatico* (1890)

A descriptive sonnet, notable for its sharp delineation of details, some of which derive from an article by Luigi Paolucci *Sulle voci degli uccelli*. Of puffins it says: 'le loro voci sono lunghe, tenute piuttosto basse, come quelle di marinai, che da una barca all'altra conversino per ingannare il tempo della bonaccia importuna: ovvero si ripetono interrotte e rapide come dolci e oziose risate' (quoted by L. M. Capelli, *Dizionarietto pascoliano*, Livorno, 1916, vol. i). The puffin belongs essentially to extreme northern latitudes as its scientific name indicates (*Fratercula arctica*), but it is vagrant as far south as the Mediterranean.

1 **carmino** 'crimson'. Literally *carmino* is cochineal extract, from which the crimson dye (*carminio*) is made. Other examples of *recherché* and technical vocabulary in the poem are: *marezzate, randa, garbino, stagliate, lacca.*

2 **recide intorno** 'circumscribes'.

marezzate 'marbled', i.e. veined with different colours.

3 **cèrula** poetic form of *cerulea*, deep blue.

4 **randa** 'sail'; strictly speaking 'gaffsail', the technical term being used to indicate precisely the shape and rig of the sail.

5 **garbino** south-west wind in the Adriatic.

8 **pende** Cf. 1.14f and note.

12 **stagliate dentro** 'clear-cut against'; *stagliarsi su* = to stand out distinctly (against a background).

l'oro e il fuoco: the yellows, oranges and reds of the dawn sky, reflected in the water near the horizon.

10. Il santuario (1890)

Another descriptive sonnet.

2 **a mezzo la scogliera** The church is situated amongst pine-trees, half-way down a rocky promontory that falls steeply to the water's edge.

4 **intercolunnii** the avenues between the rows of pines: 'intercolumniation' is the technical term for the space between the columns of a temple.

5 **palpiti** 'tremors'.

8 **fiocchi** 'wisps'; literally, locks or tufts of wool or cotton.

11 **il Carro** 'the Wain' (= the Plough = the Great Bear).

14 **uguale** 'the same', i.e. never changing.

11. Tre versi dell'Ascreo (1891)

The message of this brief didactic poem — that suffering can be a purifying experience if the sufferer has the wisdom and fortitude to make it so — is brought into association with some lines by Hesiod. The result is a vigorous new poetic image. Sapphic stanzas, consisting (unlike the Sapphics of No. **66**) of three *endecasillabi* and a *quinario* with alternate rhyme. In the *endecasillabi* the fifth syllable regularly coincides with the end of a word and may be followed by a well-marked pause.

Ascreo The farmer-poet Hesiod (*c.* 700 B.C.) lived at Ascra in Boeotia.

1—4 See Hesiod, *Works and Days*, lines 737—9. The precept occurs in a section of the poem devoted to social and religious conduct. The Italian is a literal rendering of the original Greek. Construe: *Non passar* (negative of the imperative) *l'onda di perenni fiumi a meno che tu non preghi* . . .

1 **onda** Cf. 8.8.
2 **volto a** 'looking towards'.

12. *Fides* (1890)

One of several poems (cf. *Orfano, Carrettiere*) in which the happy world of dreams or of the imagination is contrasted with the menacing world of physical reality. The poem, comprising eight *endecasillabi* ABABCCDD, uses an old verseform — the *strambotto* — belonging to the Italian folk tradition.
Fides Latin for 'Faith', 'Trust'.

1 **vespero** poetic for *sera*.
4 **lassú** in heaven.
8 **scagliasi al vento** 'battles against the wind'.

13. *Ceppo* (1897)

In Pascoli's lifetime children were still told that on Christmas eve the mother of Christ goes from house to house with the infant Jesus in her arms and sits beside the yule-log (*ceppo*) for the sake of the warmth. In this poem Mary's blessing on the household is the death of the sick woman (line 21). Metre: as in No. **12**, but with several stanzas.
Ceppo 'Christmastide' (from *ceppo di Natale*, a yule-log).

2 The full peal of bells announces the start of the Mass (*l'entrata*).
7 **bricco** an earthenware or metal jug for heating water, milk, etc.
17f **fiso/nel ceppo** 'gazing at the log'.
19 **sbracia** 'gives off a shower of sparks'.
24 **sognata** as though heard in a dream.

14. Orfano (1890)

The poem dates from the same period as *Fides*, which it resembles in manner and metrical form.
  2 **Senti** imperative: 'Listen'.

15. Il cacciatore (1892)

This little 'fable' — as Pascoli called it — is the definitive version of a poem first published in 1887 with the title *L'uccellino e il cacciatore*. It belongs to a section of *Myricae* entitled 'Le pene del poeta' and deals with the frustrations of poetic composition. The huntsman is, of course, the poet. Pascoli adapts the old madrigal form: ten *endecasillabi* are articulated as two tercets and a quatrain, ABA CBC DEDE.
  1 **un tratto** = *a un tratto* 'suddenly'.
  3 **nuota** 'is in raptures'; *nuotare* used metaphorically = 'to revel' in something.
  4 **fil di sole** 'a thin shaft of sunlight'.
  5 **bàttesela al piede** 'he brings it down at his feet'.
  6 The poet, who was full of joy (*gioiva*) in the moment of inspiration, is bitterly disappointed (*si duole*) by the outcome of his effort to capture the experience in words.

16. Arano (1886)

This poem and the eight that follow are all taken from a section of *Myricae* entitled 'L'ultima passeggiata'. They record sights and sounds of the countryside and country life and apart from a few of the later poems (e.g. Nos. 22 and 24 in this selection) lack second meanings or intellectual implications. Metre: as in No. 15.
  1 **roggio** 'russet', an archaism.
  4f Note the frequent pauses in these lines and the relatively large number of heavy stresses.
  5f **ribatte/le porche** 'is levelling the ridges', i.e. using a mattock to draw the earth down over the seeds scattered in the furrows; *porche* = the ridges of earth between the furrows.
  9 **e il pettirosso** The syntactical incompleteness of the phrase arises so naturally from the impressionistic technique that it passes almost unnoticed.

17. *Di lassú* (1892)

Literally a bird's-eye view of the countryside. An earlier version (1886) was identical except for the last verse. Metre: as in No. **15**.

2 **villa** Archaic term denoting the countryside with scattered houses.

3 **che** = *dove*.

un fil di fumo . . . vapora 'a wisp of smoke rises into the air': the image is of smoke (from a bonfire or a chimney) rising like steam; *vaporare* 'to steam' (intransitive). Cf. **30**.3f.

4f **largamente . . . mira** 'gazes down on the brown furrows stretching far and wide'; *farsi* = 'to appear'.

10 **nell'orecchio** not actually, of course, but in anticipation of the summer (cf. *in suo pensiero*, line 9).

18. *Lavandare* (1894)

Metre: as in No. **15**.

Lavandare for *lavandaie*; dialect of Romagna.

4 **gora** 'mill-stream'; the public wash-place was naturally close to a source of fresh water.

7–10 This is what the women are singing.

7 **nevica** metaphorical.

8 **paese** 'village'.

9 **come** i.e. in what a state.

10 The line is taken from a folk-song.

19. *La via ferrata* (1886)

Metre: as in No. **15**.

La via ferrata 'The railway track'.

2 **si difila** = runs in a straight line.

5 **con loro trama** metaphor from weaving: the telegraph wires supported by the arms of the telegraph poles are like the weft threads (*trama*) that are woven onto the warp. The definite article, obligatory in modern prose usage, is omitted for metrical reasons.

6 **in fuggente ordine** 'in rapid succession'.

7f Construe: *Qual femminil lamento, rombando di gemiti e d'ululi, cresce e dilegua?*

rombando 'resounding (with)'.

NOTES 145

8 **cresce e dilegua** 'rises and falls'.
10 **squillano ... al vento** 'sing shrilly in the wind'.

20. *Mezzogiorno* (1886)

Metre: as in No. **15**.

5 **pingui** 'rich'.
5f The sentence after *brontola* is in direct speech.
altri i.e. the game was superior, the sportsmen more skilful (and, perhaps, more generous).
7 **s'è beato** The beggar's contentment belies his complaint (lines 5f) that 'things aren't what they used to be'.
10 **villa** See note on **17**.2.

21. *Già dalla mattina* (1892)

Metre: as in No. **15**.

1–4 The technical terms refer to parts of the mill where the corn is being ground to make flour. The corn is emptied into a hopper (*tramoggia*), at the bottom of which is an opening (*bocchetta*) that allows the grain to drop onto the shoe (*cassetta*). This is a kind of tray, which oscillates to and fro (*dondola*), feeding the corn evenly to the mill-stones. The lower stone remains stationary, whilst the upper stone (*coperchio*) revolves on its bearing (*bronzina*). In the background is the roaring of the water that feeds the mill-race. Each object is apostrophized in turn, and the resulting sequence of imperatives (*rimbomba ... dondola* etc.) lends vigour and urgency to the description.

4 **da** 'beside'.
5 **già dalla mattina** 'ever since morning'.
7 **scrolla** 'twitches'.
8–10 **tardi ... fumerai** 'it will be late before you lie steaming on the table'.
8 **tra** literally 'between', but with the same force as colloquial English 'what with ...'; it introduces an enumeration of the operations yet to be completed before the flour becomes bread.
finire, andar bel bello i.e. finishing the grinding process and journeying slowly home with the sacks of flour.
10 **pan di cruschello** kind of wholemeal bread made from flour before the final sifting and so still containing a quantity of fine bran (*cruschello*).

22. *Carrettiere* (1894)

See the introductory note to No. **12**. Metre: as in No. **15**.

6 **carbone** charcoal, which the wagoner is bringing down from the woods on the mountainside.

9f During the Advent season shepherds in Sicily and parts of southern Italy used to play their bagpipes (*cennamella* or *ciaramella*) at dawn before shrines of the Virgin. Pascoli describes the practice in 'L'avvento': see *Prose*, i.211f.

23. *In capannello* (1886)

This little scene may owe something to a popular saying in Romagna: *Tre donn e un pignat − un marché bel e fatt* ('Three women and a cooking-pot: a regular market-place'). Metre: as in No. **15**.

1 **cancello** the level-crossing gate.

3 **le comari** 'the old wives'. In its narrow sense *comare* = 'godmother' and in some parts of Italy 'midwife', but in popular speech it was used as a form of address roughly equivalent to the antiquated English 'neighbour' or 'mother'; collectively it refers to all the women of a small community.

4−8 The language of these lines is deliberately colloquial.

4 **scrivo scrivo** 'just the same', 'exactly alike', colloquial Tuscanism from the same register as English expressions such as 'the spitting image', 'as like as two peas in a pod'.

5 **costa un occhio** 'costs the earth'.

e ce n'è stato = *eppure ce n'è stato in abbondanza*.

7 **sui venti** 'getting on for twenty'.

10 **traino** = *treno*.

24. *Il cane* (1890)

Metre: as in No. **15**.

1 **va per la sua strada** 'goes on its way'.

3 **e ... e** 'both ... and'; the subjunctive mood of *vada* is determined by the expressions of emotion in line 2.

4 **Tal** *Tale* is the correlative adjective that introduces one term of a comparison: '*quale* (as) ... *tale* (so)'.

5 **che** is here a temporal conjunction (like *quando*, but much weaker); translate 'and'.

rozzon(e) 'ungainly'.

normanno = *cavallo normanno*. Percherons from Normandy,

NOTES 147

once renowned all over Europe as draught-horses, were widely used for heavy farm work.

    6 **stampa** literally 'prints', i.e. leaves behind an imprint.
    8 **lo precorre** 'runs ahead of it'.

25. *Il mago* (1889)

One of the six poems in a section of *Myricae* entitled 'Le gioie del poeta', which complements the section 'Le pene del poeta'. The poet is a wizard who can bring whole worlds into existence through the magic power of words (*Il mago*); he helps the blind to see (*Il miracolo*), takes a naive joy in the beauties of nature (*In alto*), does not seek fame for himself (*Gloria*). Metrically akin to the modified ballad form of Nos. **4** and **5**, but using *endecasillabi* and reduced to a single stanza X ABABBX.

    1 **verziere** = *giardino*, an archaism.
verone poetic for balcony or window.
    3 **fiora** from *fiorare*, archaic form of *fiorire*, 'to flower'.

26. *Contrasto* (1894)

Contrasting views of artistic creation. The second stanza expresses the same conception of the poet's role as that found in *Il fanciullino*: he discovers the beauty latent in the world about him. Metre: similar to that of No. **25**, but every vestige of a refrain has vanished, leaving only two ballad stanzas linked by their last lines, which rhyme together.

    2 **soffio ... di lena** 'I blow hard'.
    3 **ve'** = *vedi* (imperative).
fïala 'bottle'.
    4 **sereno** 'clear' (as when applied to the sky).
    7 **vo** = *vado*.
per via 'along the road'.
    8 **solo, soletto** 'all alone'.
   10 **affino** 'I make (it) perfect'.
   11 **mi sia** = *sia*. The reflexive form *essersi* is confined to poetic usage.

27. *Ida e Maria* (1889)

The title refers to Pascoli's two sisters, who were living with him at Livorno at the time the poem was written. Metre: as in No. **11**.

1 **d'oro** golden in the lamplight.

2 **escir** = *uscir(e)*, 'to emerge (as flowers)'.

3 **bisso** fine linen (cf. *lino* in line 6); a rare word deriving from Greek βύσσος ('byssus'), the name given in the ancient world to a fabric woven from flax; used in modern poetry to emphasize the rare quality of the muslin, linen or other fine cloth referred to.

6 **rigasi** = *si riga*, 'is ruled'. The subject has changed abruptly from *mani* to *lino*, leaving the relative clause (*che . . . andando*) hanging in the air, but the sense remains clear, as though Pascoli had written: *o mani d'oro, che leggiere andando, fanno sí che il lino si righi*. A good example of the syntactical freedom (more usual in the spoken than in the written language) which Pascoli permitted himself in achieving a more relaxed, less formal style.

miracolo a vederlo another momentary change of subject as the sentence is interrupted for a parenthetical exclamation.

9 **opra** = *opera*, 'labour'.

14 **funebre panno** a shroud.

15 **però che** = *perché*.

18 **amïanto** 'amiantus', another rare word. To the mineralogist amiantus is the finest hornblende asbestos, distinguished from other kinds of asbestos by the fact that its fibres are exceptionally long and silky. Ruskin called it 'as fine and soft as any cotton thread you ever sewed with' (*Ethics of Dust*, 1866). Its properties were known to the ancient world, and the Romans used it to make lampwicks and cremation cloths. Thus the word connotes something rare, precious, delicate and indestructible.

19 **onde** depends on *grevi*: 'laden with which . . .'
pia 'loving', 'devoted'.

28 **riscintillanti** intensified form of *scintillanti*, 'brightly shining', 'brilliant'.

28. *Il vecchio dei campi* (1891)

This poem and the six that follow (Nos. **29—34**) belong to a section of *Myricae* entitled 'In campagna': another series of impressions of the countryside and country life, for the most part without second meanings. Metre: as in No. **11**.

7f **far sacca ... delle lenzuola.** The old man recalls a year when his vegetable crop was so heavy that, in order to transport it, extra sacks had to be made out of sheets.

11 **Rondello** Buovo's faithful horse Arundel.

12 **Buovo d'Antona** (= Bevis of Hampton) hero of famous thirteenth-century chivalrous romances (in both French and English) which, like a number of similar legends, owe their wide diffusion and continued popularity in Italy to the version in *I reali di Francia*, a compilation of Carolingian stories made by the Florentine *cantastorie* Andrea da Barberino in the fifteenth century. The episode alluded to (lines 11f) is recounted in Book IV at the end of chapter 12.

29. *Nella macchia* (1894)

The landscape here described (the *macchia del Limone*) is that of the Tuscan Maremma near Livorno, which provided the setting for many of the *Myricae*. The 'madrigal' form is similar to that of No. **15**, except for the use of a *quaternario* in lines 10 and 20 and the replacement elsewhere of *endecasillabi* by *novenari*.

2 **stipe** *Stipa pennata*, feather grass.

9f *Sbuffare* (literally 'to pant', 'to puff') is used of the chuffing noise of steam-engines; *ringhio* (literally 'snarling') is usually used of dogs or other animals. Together with *argentini* they form a seemingly impossible constellation of words, but are effective in suggesting the familiar 'tea-cher tea-cher' call of the Great Tit described by Pascoli elsewhere in similar terms: 'striduli *sbuffi* ... che sembrano piccoli *nitriti* chiusi in gola d'uccello' ('Il sabato' in *Prose*, i.59).

14 **fosco** in the gloom.

20 In the glossary he compiled for *Canti di Castelvecchio* Pascoli wrote: 'Tutte [le mie soavi lettrici] sanno ... che il merlo (e anche la capinera) fischia *Io ti vedo*.' The blackbird's song is similarly characterized in 'Il fanciullino' (*Prose*, i.46).

30. *Dall'argine* (1891)

Metre: as in No. **11**.

3 **biancica** = *biancheggia*, 'appears white'.

3f **via via/fila** 'it drifts upwards in a fine thread' (*filare* literally = 'to form long threads'). Cf. **17**.3.

31. *Temporale* (1894)

A good example of colour impressionism. There is only one verb in the whole poem (*rosseggia*), and that could easily be replaced by an adjective of colour. Metre: as in No. 25, but using *settenari*.

   3 **a mare** 'out at sea'.
   4 **a monte** 'over the mountain'.

32. *Dopo l'acquazzone* (1891)

Metre: as in No. 11.
   7 **uno stuolo** a band of children.
   8 **bomba** 'base' in a children's game.

33. *Pioggia* (1894)

Each of the descriptive details in lines 1—4 alludes to a popular belief concerning signs of rain: cocks crowing before dawn, the croaking of frogs and crows, the face of the sun cut in two by a layer of cloud. Metre: as in No. 25, but with two stanzas.

   3 **a finestrelle** 'fitfully'.
   5 **a catinelle** 'in bucketfuls', 'cats and dogs'. Cf. the proverb: 'Sole a finestrelle, acqua a catinelle'.
   9 The image of rain falling like 'pins' produces a combined audio-visual effect.
   10 **sorsate** 'lapping sounds'.
   11 **chiazze** puddles or patches of rain-soaked earth.
picchi the miniature 'peaks' raised by rain-drops falling into puddles. (Some commentators prefer to take *picchi* as plural of *picchio* = a tapping sound.)
a mille a mille 'by their thousands'.

34. *Novembre* (1891)

Metre: as in No. 11.
   1 **Gemmea** 'crystalline', 'crystal-clear' (literally, 'gem-like'); suppression of the verb *essere* makes the construction elliptical.
   2—4 It feels like spring.
   5 **pruno** any thorny shrub, but in particular *pruno selvatico* (= blackthorn or sloe, *Prunus spinosa*) or *pruno gazzerino* (= firethorn, *Pyracantha coccinea*) might be found in the hedge alongside hawthorn.

NOTES 151

5–9   Note the long series of alliterations and assonances using the consonant *s* and the vowel *e*. The repeated sibilant, thanks to the key words *secco* and *stecchite*, gives rise to a tactile sensation of dryness, whilst the assonances produce a general effect of melodiousness.

6   **trame**   the intricate patterns made by the interlaced branches.

7   **piè** = *piede.*

7–11   A new series of assonances, based on the vowel-sound *o*, begins with *vuoto*, whose meaning determines the nature of the sound effect produced.

11–12   Alliteration returns, giving rise to a combination of aural and tactile sensations, the precise quality of which depends on the words *fragile* and *fredda.*

35. Lo stornello (1887)

An early sonnet.

Lo stornello   'The Song'. Pascoli uses the term in a general sense to mean any kind of simple folk-song. More precisely, what the unseen serenader of the poem is singing is a *rispetto* (see line 3), a version of which was collected and published by Tommaseo in *Canti toscani*, Venice, 1841, p. 384. The folk-song tradition was still alive at the time of the poem's composition. Such songs might accompany agricultural operations such as threshing, maize-stripping, etc., which involved groups of workers.

3   **tale**   'thus'.

rispetto   the Tuscan name for an old form of folk-song, usually comprising six or eight *endecasillabi*, but occasionally only four; so called because the song was an expression of homage to the loved one. It was just one variety of the *strambotto* (see introductory note to No. 12).

5   **quasi arguta spola**   'like a shrill-sounding shuttle'; a cliché of Latin poetry.

6   **un bruire**   'a rustling', archaic.

esile e schietto   i.e. faint but distinct. In prose usage *esile* (literally 'slender', 'thin') may be applied to voices; *schietto* literally = 'pure', 'plain', 'simple'.

8   **le rincresce**   'she regrets'.

9   **là dalla siepe** = *al di là della siepe*, 'beyond the hedge'.

12   **a stella a stella**   'star by star'.

36. Benedizione (1888)

Another early composition, the form of which derives from the *sonetto caudato* (sonnet with a tail). The lines are *ottonari* except for line 15 (a *quaternario*), which provides the link with the final couplet constituting the 'tail'.

   10 **sí ... e sí** 'both ... and'.

   12 **falco** The Italian word is applied not only to falcons, but also to hawks, harriers, kestrels and other birds of prey in the family of the *Falconidae*. Pascoli could mean the black kite (*falco nero*); at all events the context suggests that the species alluded to lacks the noble associations attaching to English 'falcon'.

falchetto the young of the *falco*.

37. Con gli angioli (1894)

According to Pascoli himself 'Ridi con gli angioli' was a local expression in Romagna commonly addressed to anyone seen to smile for no apparent reason. It was believed that such a person would soon die. Another local superstition, adding further meaning to the poem, was that a girl who made her own bridal gown would not live long enough to enjoy her happiness. In content the poem is comparable with No. 6. Its form is that of the *strambotto*: as No. 12, but with the rhyme-scheme ABABABAB.

   1 **ulivelle** The *ulivella* or *olivella* is the spurge laurel (*Daphne laureola*), a spring-flowering wild plant, faintly scented.

   3 It is evening. The stars, likened to the buds (*bocci*) of nocturnal flowers, are not yet out, but are waiting for the night air to 'open' them.

   4 **mimosa** the Sensitive Plant (*Mimosa pudica*), the behaviour of whose leaves is described in Shelley's poem of that name: 'it opened its fan-like leaves to the light, / And closed them beneath the kisses of night.'

38. Mare (1891)

Metre: as in No. 12.

   1 Several Umbrian folk-songs begin with this line.

39. Il nido (1889)

Another early sonnet.

   3 **riviera** In modern Italian the word is restricted to mean a stretch of coast, but in early Italian it could refer to a river or to the countryside, as here.

   4 **convito** used in the now obsolete sense of diners at a banquet; translate 'company'.

   9 **già** used here as an intensifying adverb expressing both affirmation and regret: *già . . . ora* 'now alas'.

  10 **concento** 'harmony'. Like *riviera* and *convito* the word belongs to an elevated literary style.

40. Il lampo (1894)

Metre: as in No. **25**.

   2 **in sussulto** 'shaking violently'.
   3 **ingombro** heavy with clouds.

41. Il tuono (1900)

Metre: as in No. **25**.

   4 Only two of the syllables are unstressed; the other nine carry either a heavy or an intermediate stress.

   5 **rimareggiò** 'swelled up again'.
   6 **vaní** archaic form of *svaní* 'faded away'.

42. La baia tranquilla (1894)

The escapist mood and rapid movement of this poem are reminiscent of some of the lighthearted erotic verse of the eighteenth century. Metre: as in No. **36**.

   6 **di là da** 'from beyond'.
   8 **marinaia** 'sailor's wife'.

43. La Sirena (1894)

The title alludes to the sea-nymphs of Greek mythology, whose songs lured to destruction the sailors who listened to them (see particularly *Odyssey*, xii). In the poem, however, the *sirena* is a fog-horn, exercising the same fatal magic. Metre: *novenari* in quatrains with alternate rhyme. With the exception of lines 1 and 14 all the *novenari* have a regular dactylo-anapaestic rhythm.

12ff   The viewpoint is that of the passengers aboard the ship, whose thoughts return to the shore they have left behind and the familiar sights and sounds of home.

13f   **che scese/già** 'which has already sunk'. Past historic used in imitation of the Latin perfect tense.

PRIMI POEMETTI

All the *Poemetti* — 'Primi' and 'Nuovi' alike — are in *terza rima*, so that in respect of metre at least the two collections are more homogeneous than *Myricae*. The same is true up to a point of the content of the collections, because six of the sections comprising the two volumes were originally planned as a single cycle of poems dealing with rural life and occupations, and from this arose the common practice of referring to the *Poemetti* as Pascoli's *Georgics*. The sections are the ones entitled: 'La sementa' and 'L'accestire' (both in *Primi poemetti*), 'La fiorita' and 'La mietitura' (both in *Nuovi poemetti*), 'Il vecchio castagno' (*Primi poemetti*) and 'I filugelli' (*Nuovi poemetti*). The setting for this cycle is the Garfagnana, as the region around Castelvecchio is called: the protagonists of the narrative had their real-life counterparts among the poet's acquaintances, and the language, which in some passages uses numerous technical terms, also draws freely on the local dialect. It will be seen, however, from the poems chosen for this selection (Nos. **44—52**) that, leaving aside the rustic sequence, the content of the *Poemetti* is as diversified as that of the *Myricae*; but the style is predominantly narrative (or narrative-descriptive), a fact which helps to explain the choice of metre. The division of the *Poemetti* into 'Primi' and 'Nuovi' is explained in the Introduction.

44. *Il vischio* (1896)

It is customary to regard the mistletoe of the poem as symbolizing evil, but this interpretation adds very little to the poem's literal significance as a representation of the deadly strength of the parasite. The metre is that of all the *Poemetti: terza rima*.

NOTES

1 **ricordi** The imaginary listener addressed in the 2nd person singular is the *anima sorella* of line 27.

2–4 The peach and plum blossom is likened to pink and white clouds.

4–6 The rest of the sentence is elliptical: a catalogue of impressions without any verb.

4 **pendula** The adjective has been transferred from *fiocchi* 'tassels'.

9 **improvvisa** 'unexpected', i.e. unexpectedly, almost miraculously suffused for days on end with the colours of the dawn sky.

11 **quella** refers back to *alba*.

11–13 The poet, distilling sweetness and sustenance from his illusions, is likened to a bee making honey from pollen.

12 **pasceva già l'illusïone** 'was already feeding on illusion'. **ond'** = *onde*, 'from which'.

18 **per** 'in'.

19 Cf. **53**.14.

23 **branche** literally 'claws', here used figuratively of the open petals.

24 **su l'aurora** 'at daybreak'.

27 **anima sorella** almost certainly refers to the poet's sister, but the expression could be understood in a wider sense as 'kindred spirit'. Romantic poets had used *sorella* to mean 'soul-mate'.

29f **qualche cosa anche piú bella/della vita** the contemplation of beauty; aesthetic experiences in general. Cf. Pascoli's *discorso* of 1901, 'Il settimo giorno': 'Ma c'è un superfluo che nella vita è piú necessario di ciò che è necessario: la poesia. Ve lo insegnano le bambine che domandano *u sciuri* [= *i fiori*] e non domandano il pane' (*Prose*, i.241).

31 **ali** another allusion to the flower-petals.
pianta 'tree'.

32 **sizïenti** 'thirsty'; an archaism.

33 **già diede** Cf. *scese già* (**43**.13f).

34 **questa** the fruit-tree (*pianta*), which has become the host for the parasitic mistletoe.

38 **quella** the same sterile tree as the one indicated in 34f.

40 **ignoto** no longer recognizable as a fruit-tree of any known species.

42 **due verdi** the green of the tree and the green of the

mistletoe, which has a yellowish tinge (*un gialleggiar*).

43 **tristo** 'ill-fated', 'accursed'.

44 **foglie diverse** the leaves of the fruit-tree and those of the mistletoe.

45 **glomi** 'globes', alluding to the shape of the mistletoe bushes, which grow in rounded clusters; a Latinism derived from *glomus* = a ball, e.g. of wool.

trame 'tangled clusters'; cf. **34**.6.

53—5 Readers who take the mistletoe as a symbolic image will interpret these lines as a question about the origin of evil.

56 Either the tree did not know (*non sapeva*) what was happening to it, or else it did not believe (*non credeva*) that such a thing could happen.

ei = *egli* (*il vischio*).

66f **Senti/piú** 'Can you any longer feel . . .?'

67 **quando mai t'affisi**: 'If you study yourself'; *affisare* is a poetic form of *fisare*; subjunctive mood.

74f **Tu vivi l'altra . . . t'involi/da te** 'Your life is that of the other . . . you are growing away from yourself'; *l'altra* (*anima*) = that of the mistletoe; *t'involi* = *t'allontani*.

77 **checché gemmasti allora** 'whatever buds you may have produced in the past'; *gemmare* is normally intransitive.

45. *Digitale purpurea* (1898)

A poem about the destructive power of sexual passion symbolized by the foxglove, here represented as a maleficent plant with a deadly fragrance. It is from this plant (*Digitalis purpurea*) that the substance digitalis is obtained: in small quantities it is a heart-stimulant; in large doses a poison. When Maria Pascoli was a schoolgirl at Sogliano, she and her friends saw foxgloves for the first time in a garden near the convent: 'La Madre Maestra ci intimò . . . di non appressarci a quel fiore che emanava un profumo venefico e cosí penetrante che faceva morire' (*Lungo la vita di G. Pascoli*, p. 134). The foxglove symbol has been variously interpreted. For some interesting analyses of the poem see: E. Cecchi, *La poesia di Giovanni Pascoli*, Milan, 1968, 63—72; G. Getto, *Carducci e Pascoli*, Bologna, 1957, 131—52; G. Barberi Squarotti, *Simboli e strutture della poesia del Pascoli*, Messina—Florence, 1966, 153—60; C. Distante, *Giovanni Pascoli poeta inquieto tra '800 e '900*, Florence, 1968, 153—7. *Terza rima*.

1ff   As so often in Pascoli's poetry the reader must supply the details of the *mise en scène* that are adumbrated in the poem without being made explicit. The two girls are reviving memories of their days together at the convent school. Maria, in whom Pascoli commemorates his sister, still retains her childhood innocence, but her friend has inhaled the deadly scent of the flower of passion.

L'una = Maria; **l'altra** = Rachele.

19   **come un miele**   'a sort of honey'.

35f   **quale** belongs with *ospite*: 'what welcome visitor?' **grate**: the window in the *parlatorio*, where the nuns converse with visitors through a grille.

41ff   The distinction between past and present is deliberately blurred. *Piangono* relates to the present situation (the girls engaged in nostalgic reminiscence), but the garden 'white with young girls' in white dresses is the convent garden of their childhood, a recollection of the *cari anni lontani* (line 53); there is nothing in the syntax to mark the transition.

44   **ciarliero**   full of the sound of chattering voices.

44f   **col suono/di vele al vento**   The rustling of habits and the fluttering noise of starched linen head-dresses are likened to the sound of flapping sails (*vele*).

48f   **dita/spruzzolate di sangue**   The pinkish-purple flowers of the foxglove are sometimes marked with spots on the inside.

50   **ignoto**   'secret', 'mysterious'; literally, 'unknown'.

54   **sa**   'is aware'.

55   **tristo e pio**   'melancholy and full of tender feeling'.

56   'the taking of a last farewell'; *lontanare* (archaic) = *allontanarsi*, 'to recede into the distance'.

61   **cetonie**   rose-beetles (*Cetonia aurata*).

64   **che notturno arse**   'which smouldered during the night'.

71   **dirmi sentia**   'I heard a voice say to me'.

73f   **lo stupore/alza degli occhi**   'raises her eyes in amazement'.

46. Suor Virginia (1903)

Pascoli rarely managed to handle the theme of death without melodrama or mawkishness, but he does so here. Equally successful is his unsentimental portrayal of piety and meekness in the figure of the old nun, whose divine simplicity makes her

158   NOTES

a sister in spirit to the protagonist of a contemporary poem, Paolo Uccello (see No. **68**). The mysterious nocturnal atmosphere contributes much to the total effect of the poem, which — like No. **45** — originated in an anecdote of Maria Pascoli's about her life in the Augustinian convent-school at Sogliano. See *Lungo la vita di G. Pascoli*, pp. 132f. *Terza rima*.

5 **di nulla** i.e. *perdono di nulla*: she had committed no sin requiring forgiveness.

5f Cf. Psalm 123.2: 'Behold, as the eyes of servants look unto the hand of their masters, and as the eyes of a maiden unto the hand of her mistress; so our eyes wait upon the Lord our God'.

7 **a una** depends on *simile* (line 5).

8 **socchiuso** qualifies *uscio* (line 7).

9 **ch'altri non oda** 'so that no one may hear'.

11 i.e. before a representation of the agony of Santa Rita, who is portrayed in Catholic iconography as praying before a crucifix, wearing a crown of thorns. Sister Virginia appears to imitate the attitude of the saint.

Santa Rita: an Augustinian nun (1381–1457) from Umbria, who endured with exceptional fortitude the strain of a chronic and painful malady.

16 **Si rimise in dosso** 'She put on again'.

17 **scapolare** The scapular consists of two strips of cloth hanging down the breast and back, and joined across the shoulders.

17f **Forse ... stanza** Someone (she supposes) may be trying to attract her attention by knocking on the wall of the dormitory next door. In Maria Pascoli's anecdote it was she who tapped on the wall to draw someone's attention to the open window (line 24), but Sister Virginia had such a reputation for severity that the child feigned sleep when the nun entered the dormitory.

19 **qualche educanda** one of the boarders at the convent-school.

22 **nel lor guscio** i.e. closed; the eyelids are likened to the skin of a fruit, or the shell or husk of a nut.

31 **sgnaulío** The word (more usually *gnaulío*) is onomatopoeic in origin. Pascoli extends its application from the sound made by cats to similar whining or screeching noises.

34 **d'appiatto** = *di nascosto* 'stealthily'.

35 **represso** past participle of *reprimere*: 'restrained'.

NOTES

43 **nell'alta notte** 'in the dead of night'.

56 'she heard a pin drop on the floor'.

63f **raccolta/al ... sonno** 'gathered in the arms of sleep'.

65f **s'era ... rivolta/sul cuore** 'had turned over on her left side'.

67 **il Santo** = San Pasquale: 'il santo i suoi devoti li avverte tre giorni prima [della morte] affinché si preparino' (M. Pascoli, *op cit.*, p. 133).

69 **Val** = *Valle* 'Vale (of tears)'.

71 **pater** the Lord's prayer, which in Latin begins 'Pater noster'.

71f The world may be vast (*ampia*), but the Saint knows (*non ignora*) where each of us lives (*il nostro limitare*).

75 **ospite** The underlying image seems to be that of people as guests at the banquet of life.

85f Literally, the time had come when 'Suor Virginia must pack up her life and depart'; *fardello* = 'bundle'; *far f.* = 'to pack up (all one's possessions) and leave'.

87 **il suo fardello** The full force of the phrase becomes apparent in the next sentence, which explains it.

89ff The dying nun's vision is of the martyred virgin Saint Ursula and her companions. (The actual number of women with Ursula when she arrived in Cologne in A.D. 453 was eleven; the legendary number of 11,000 derives from an erroneous interpretation of the inscription on her tomb, the letter M being taken to mean *mille* instead of *martyres*.) The Ursuline order, the oldest and most considerable teaching order of women in the Roman Catholic church, was founded in 1535 for the purpose of educating young girls.

93f The bowl-shaped vessels (*conche*) carried by the virgins are made of translucent material (*alabastro*), through which gleams the mellow light of their lamps (*le lor dolci vite*). The imagery comes from Foscolo's *Le grazie*, 'Inno Secondo': *Recate insieme, o vergini, le conche/dell'alabastro provvido di fresca/linfa e di vita* (lines 113–15 in Gavazzeni's edition, Ricciardi, 1974).

98f **come gli Ave.../corona** 'like the Hail Marys of a rosary, one bead (*grano*) after another'.

100 **di sotto.** 'from under'.

101 **stole** 'robes'; the *stola* was the long flowing garment worn by Roman matrons.

105 **che** 'whilst'.

tuttavia = *ancora* 'still'.

106 **splendean ... per la terra** The last figures in the long line of martyrs were still walking on the earth, although the leaders were already approaching the gates of heaven.
per: 'along'.

111 **Di là** in the dormitory, where the child is knocking for the fourth time.

47. La quercia caduta (1900)

It is customary to regard the felling of the oak-tree as a metaphor for the unjust assassination of the poet's father; but this interpretation, so far from illuminating the poem, unnecessarily restricts its significance as a comment on life's injustices and the egotistic behaviour of the generality of people. *Terza rima*.

1 **sé** object of *spande*.

5 **nidïetti** diminutive formed from the archaic form *nidio* (= *nido* 'nest').

48. La siepe (1897)

A farmer praises the hedge that surrounds his land and keeps out unwelcome intruders. The poem is one of nine dealing with country life and occupations, and joined loosely in a cycle entitled 'L'accestire'. It is the best of the group and loses nothing by being read in isolation. The hedge as a symbol of private ownership occurs also in d'Annunzio's election speech of 1897 known as 'La siepe'. The composition of Pascoli's poem goes back to 1889. *Terza rima*.

1 **campetto** The more usual diminutive form is *campicello*.

pia As so often in the language of Italian poetry (cf. Carducci's 'pio bove'), it means 'loyal', 'trusty', 'serviceable'; from Latin *pius* in its most general sense of 'acting according to duty'.

3 **che dice mia** The hedge proclaims the farmer's ownership of the field, as the ring on the finger of a wife.

che fu mia not just 'who belonged to me', but 'whom I possessed' (in the sexual sense).

8 **al ladro dormi 'l-dí** 'to the nocturnal thief'; *un dormi* = a sleepy person, and *un ladro dormi 'l-dí* is a thief who sleeps during the daytime.

13 *siepe* understood: (*siepe*) *d'albaspina* . . .
15 **per te** 'because of you'. Also in line 21.
22 'she harvests the fruit of the teeming cherry-tree'; *miete* literally 'reaps'; *popolosi* = 'densely populated' (i.e. with fruit).
23—6 Note the free syntax, which a poet like Carducci would have found intolerable. The verb *dice* (line 23) is repeated in line 26, leaving the intervening lines to form a kind of parenthesis.
25 **che** serves here as a weak temporal conjunction (= 'whilst'); translate 'and'.
26 **se t'aggrada** = *se ti piace*, 'if you want to', 'when it pleases you'.
27 **correggi** 'train' (literally, 'correct').
per il pioppo 'along the poplar-tree', which is being used to support the vine.
29 **per lei** Cf. note on line 15.
33 **tu pur(e)** 'you too'.
35 **dici un divieto** 'you pronounce a warning against entry'.
37 **forte ad altrui . . . a me pia** 'strong against others . . . loyal to me'; cf. line 1.
38 **fede** 'wedding-ring', repeating the idea of the hedge as a ring and the field as a wife (lines 2f).
ori: 'jewels'.
39 Cf. line 3.

49. Nella nebbia (1897)

This descriptive poem, in the same metre as the preceding ones, may be compared with No. 55 (*Nebbia*); also with one not included in this selection entitled *In cammino* (*Myricae*), in which the mist is made to serve as a symbolic metaphor of man's ignorance and inability to grasp the meaning of life. The present composition has no symbolic or allegorical import.
3 **unito** 'uniform'.
5 **vocío** normally used of human voices (= a constant shouting), but here applied to the screaming of birds.
8 **sogni di rovine** i.e. insubstantial, like dreams.
11 **donde** 'for what reason'.

50. *Il libro* (1896)

This poem is similar in style to *Il vischio*, but is overtly allegorical. Its theme is man's restless and unsuccessful striving to comprehend the mystery of the universe and of human existence. *Terza rima*.

1 **altana** A common feature of houses in the Mediterranean is a roof-terrace, balcony or loggia, where one can sit out of doors during the summer.

2–5 The syntax is reduced to bare essentials. The book was already ancient before the oak-tree, destined to provide material for the book-rest, had been felled.

3 **esercitata** 'buffeted'.

4 **selva** synonymous with *foresta*, but from a higher level of diction; moreover its use in preference to the more familiar word makes possible an elegant alliterative effect. Cf. *fragili fogli* in line 18.

7 **donde mai?** 'where ever from?'

8 **cui** = *che*. See note on 7.6.

13 **invisibile ... come il pensiero** 'invisible ... like thought'.

15 **estrema** = *ultima*.

29 **chimere** 'fancies', 'figments of the imagination'.

31 **tumidi** The image is of canvas bulging in the wind.

33 **sacra** 'awesome'.

34f **canti/lunghi ... come di sirene** These siren voices resemble the celestial fanfares which, in the poem *In cammino*, summon the weary pilgrim (= mankind) to continue his journey towards a vague and distant destination or ideal.

51. *Il transito* (1897)

A spectacular description of the southerly migration of the whooper swan during the arctic winter. The eery, supernatural atmosphere is the result of associations attaching to certain key words and phrases. *Transito* ('passage') can also mean death or transcendence, whilst the first sentence of the poem evokes, consciously or otherwise, the notion of 'swansong', the legendary last song of the so-called 'mute' swan before it dies; thus the swan in the poem might be thought of as setting out on a last flight through the *portici profondi* that open up in front of it in line 15. The total effect of the poem depends on these calculated ambiguities, which operate subliminally even before they are consciously recognized.

Various symbolic interpretations have been suggested, but they all seem to lessen rather than enhance the splendid suggestiveness of the poem. *Terza rima*.

1   **Il cigno canta**   The *cigno selvatico* or whooper swan nests in the Arctic tundra and migrates as far south as the Mediterranean. Its flight-call (likened in the poem first to the clashing of cymbals, then to the metallic twanging of harps and finally to the pealing of bells) is a loud trumpeting.
lame: 'tundra'.

6   **póntano**   'press down on'; an archaism.
lastrico   The frozen sea is like the paved surface of a road.

7f   **il cielo/sfuma nel buio**   'the sky vaporizes in the darkness'. So begins the description of the spectacular atmospheric phenomenon known as the Aurora Borealis or northern lights. More details are added in the three *terzine* that follow.

11   **tintina** = *tintinna* 'rings'.
13   **ne** refers to *arco* in the following line.
14   **iridato** = *iridescente* 'rainbow-coloured'.
19   **un rintocco di campana** 'a bell-note'.
20   **ultimo** 'for the last time'.
22   **nella luce boreale** 'under the northern lights'.

NUOVI POEMETTI

52. La pecorella smarrita (1906)

Of all the heavenly bodies in the universe, Earth alone is evil and in need of redemption; it is therefore the part of the universe most dear to God. The parable of the lost sheep (see Luke, xv. 3–7) is here invested with cosmic significance. The subject of the poem was suggested to the poet by the same Franciscan friend (Fr Teodosio da San Detole) to whom *Paulo Ucello* had been dedicated. *Terza rima*.

1ff   Cf. note on **45**.1ff. The thoughts and experiences here described are those of an imaginary monk, woken from sleep by a supernatural voice.

5   As dawn comes up in the east, the darkness seems to drain away below the western horizon.

6   **Biancica** = *Biancheggia* 'shows white' (in the light of dawn).

10   **"Si dirompe il cielo!"**   ' "The sky is bursting open!" ' — as though the night sky were a dark film which splits open

to allow the dawn light to stream through (cf. The English metaphor 'at break of day'). Taken at this level the words describe a familiar daily phenomenon; but to the eyes of the monk it is the dawning of the Day of Judgment, the end of the world. To him the material universe is literally disintegrating and flowing away, to be replaced by God's presence: 'God is dawning'.

11f **Plaudite con le mani** ' "Clap your hands" ', etc. The language is vaguely biblical as befits the account of an apocalyptic vision.

12 **Hermon ... Carmelo** Mt Hermon is the highest mountain in Palestine. Snow usually lies on the summit all year, causing plentiful dews (cf. Psalms, cxxxiii.3) and feeding the river Jordan as it melts. Mt Carmel is situated on the Mediterranean coast of Palestine just south of the Bay of Acre. In the Old Testament it is a by-word for luxuriant fertility (cf. Isaiah, xxv.2; Song of Songs, vii.5). The two localities have been selected for the exceptional qualities that distinguish them from the arid regions surrounding them.

14 **squittíano** = *squittivano*; cf. note on **4**.7.

le sei ali see Isaiah, vi. 2. In Catholic theology the seraphim are the highest order of angels.

15 **vedea** See note on **4**.7.

17 **Su lui** 'Above him'.

17f The imagery of line 5 is continued with a metaphor of river movement.

19 **l'avvento** At one level 'Advent', at the other level 'the second coming (of Christ)'.

23 **duce** 'Master'. Literally *duce* = 'leader' (Latin *dux*); *il sommo duce* is God.

27 Names of stars.

32 **tristo** for *triste* 'sad', as in **45**.55; for a more common use of *tristo* see **44**.43.

33 **perché ... si sveli** 'that (the whole mystery) should be revealed'.

35f '... you are not one thing and the heavens another' (i.e. you are not unique, not the fixed centre of a geocentric universe); *che* is a weak consecutive conjunction ('so that'); the mood of *siano* is determined by the negative in the principal clause. The highly expressive phrase owes its intensity to the linguistic economy, which in turn results from the loose colloquial syntax.

36 **Non, del tuo Signor, sei l'orto** The sense is 'Non sei l'orto del tuo Signor', but the Italian word order gives such prominence to the words *del tuo Signor* that they acquire causal force: 'because you are the Lord's'.

37 **a fiori ... a steli** 'as flowers ... as stalks'.

41 **cui** = *di cui*.

trastulla: intransitive, instead of the more usual reflexive form.

47 **un villaggio** Bethlehem, birthplace of Christ.

57f Note the free syntax. Normal prose usage would require: *di cui il pastor buono non s'affanna*. Pascoli achieves a more spontaneous effect equivalent to: *ripensò quelle tante pecorelle [che ci sono], eppure il pastor buono non di lor s'affanna*.

64 'The only place in the holy mountain where there is killing'. For the 'holy mountain' as a metaphor for the universe, see Isaiah, xi.9: 'They shall not hurt or destroy in all my holy mountain.'

66 **tristi lagrime** 'bitter tears', 'tears of grief and pain'.

71 **nell'alta notte** See **46**.43.

73 **dal mal pensiero** 'evil-minded', 'with evil thoughts'.

80 **folgorío** 'glittering'.

82 **la Polare** = *la stella polare* 'the pole star'.

85 **seco** = *con sé*.

88 **colassú** = *colà* + *su* = 'up there'.

90 **la zampogna pastorale** 'the shepherd's pipe'.

91 **la cerula pendice** 'the blue slopes of heaven'.

91—3 The lines apply with equal force and meaning both to the Incarnation and to the second coming of Christ. The time perspective has been telescoped.

CANTI DI CASTELVECCHIO

The thematic material of this collection is the same as that of *Myricae*, but the subject-matter is explored at greater length, in poems of greater metrical complexity, with more attention to musical effects.

53. La poesia (1897)

The poem is a sort of manifesto stating what poetry should be about (the familiar aspects and experiences of everyday life) and enumerating its aims: to illuminate, to gladden the heart, to kindle affection and devotion, to keep alive the memory of the dead, but above all to unite and console. Each stanza of 18 lines is divided into two sections of 5 lines (similar in structure and rhyme-scheme) and a longer section of 8 lines, the syntax being carefully adapted to the internal divisions of the stanza. *Novenari* are interspersed with *trisillabi* (lines 2, 7 and 18 of each stanza) and *senari* (lines 5 and 10 of each stanza). The two *senari*, rhyming together, link the first two sections of each stanza; alternate rhyme elsewhere: $Ab_3 ABX_6 : Cd_3 CDX_6 : EFEFGHGh_3$. The comparative amplitude and complexity of the stanzas, whilst reminiscent of the *canzone*, may derive from a much older model, the Pindaric ode, to which Pascoli was evidently alluding when he described the poem as 'un inno triadico alla poesia'.

1 **arda** subjunctive: 'a lamp [of a kind] that will burn softly'.

5 **veglia** an old form of *vecchia* 'an old woman'.

6 **ragioni** = *discorsi* 'conversation'.

9 **soffici**. The adjective refers to the fluffy wool or flax on the distaff (*rocca*).

14 Cf. **44**.19.

17f 'to the accompaniment of the quiet, peaceful chewing of the oxen'; in the kind of farmhouse imagined here the stalls for the animals adjoin the living quarters.

21 **sboccia** 'bursts' (like a flower-bud); for a similar use of the image of light appearing like a bud opening, see **37**.3.

24 **convito** people at the supper-table. Cf. **39**.4.

28 **beve** i.e. from the ink-well. Possibly Pascoli had in mind an old riddle of the nursery: 'Qual è quell'oggetto che corre e beve?'

30 **nel tempo che** 'whilst'.

37 **Se già non ... io sia** 'Unless, of course, I am ...' Cf. **39**.9 for a similar use of *già* as intensifying adverb.

39 **una dolce Maria** a statue or picture of the Virgin Mary at a wayside shrine.

40f **vivendo ... capanne** The lamp is fed with oil supplied by numerous poor cottagers.

44 **villa** (archaic) 'village'.

46 **sonante di canne** 'rustling with reeds'.

47 **incende** (archaic) 'sets on fire'; the light from the

lamp makes the tear-drop sparkle in the eye of the person praying at the shrine.

49   **ciglio** (poetic) 'eye'.

55   **velata** shaded so as not to disturb the sleeping woman.

63   'voyages across the sea of life'.

67f   **tenaci ... sorrisi** 'unchanging smiles'. The fair-haired maidens, like the old men and the mother, are in their graves.

69   **ombra senz'ore** 'eternal darkness'.

72   **róso**: 'consumed by grief', but the literal sense of *roso* cannot be entirely suppressed. The macabre ambiguity is not accidental: parallel instances occur in other poems, e.g. *La voce*, **57**.26.

78   **Ch'io penda** 'Whether I hang ...'

84   **trita** 'treads'.

85   **notturno** 'at night'.

54. Il compagno dei taglialegna (1905)

The poem retells a popular story about how the robin came by his red breast. Six-line stanzas consisting of alternating *novenari* and *ottonari* ABACBC. Lines 4 and 6 of each stanza are *versi tronchi*.

1   **lombardi** 'The name *Lombards* is given to men from the region of Modena who live in the mountains separating them from the *toschi* (as they call the people of Tuscany). They are tall, well-built, fair-haired people with blue eyes: true *Longobards*. They are poor and robust. They come to Tuscany every year, then travel about the islands and even as far as Africa, cutting timber and squaring it' (translation of Pascoli's own note).

4   The line must be read without synaloepha between the onomatopoeic *sci* and the vowel following, with which it is in hiatus.

5   **l'Alpe loro** 'their mountains', although the Italian noun is singular.

7   **A due a due** 'In pairs'.

tra il vento 'standing in the wind'.

9   **scento** (dialect) 'poorly dressed'.

10   **la gioventú** 'the young man'.

11   'Come on, work those powerful arms!' *Forza!* and *Su, forza!* are common expressions of encouragement in the colloquial language.

13 **pittiere** (vernaculars of Florence and other parts of Tuscany) = *pettirosso* 'robin'.

17 **richiamo** 'song', 'call'.

19 **Il Santo** St Joseph. The scene changes abruptly to Nazareth.

piombare 'to mark out' preparatory to squaring up by cutting. Literally, 'to plumb' = to check for verticality using a plumb-line, but here the carpenter is using his line to mark the wood of a felled tree-trunk. Red ochre is applied to the cord, which is stretched tightly along the wood, then plucked to leave the desired mark. See lines 25f.

26 **sinopia** 'sinoper': a kind of red clay used as a pigment, originally brought from Sinope in Asia Minor.

31 **girello** the grooved disc or spool on which the line is wound.

32 **per** 'along'.

33 **bel bello** 'carefully'.

34 **batterlo su** literally, 'to slap it (down) on (the wood)'.

37 **netto** 'suddenly'.

38 **torto venne** 'turned out crooked'.

48 **esule tribú** 'band of exiles' (the 'Lombards').

55. Nebbia (1899)

Unlike the descriptive composition *Nella nebbia* (No. **49**), this poem explores a subjective experience, and the descriptive details are unimportant in themselves. Painful thoughts and memories (of the dead members of the family) must be kept at bay and prevented from disturbing the serenity of the poet's secure little world of familiar objects. Six-line stanzas composed of *novenari* except for line 4 (a *trisillabo*) and line 6 (a *senario*) of each stanza. Rhyme scheme: $XABa_3 Bx_6$.

1 **Nascondi** imperative, as elsewhere in the poem.

4 **su** Cf. 44.24.

8 **quello ch'è morto!** It would not be wrong to see this as entailing an allusion to the poet's father, but the expression is all-embracing: not just 'him who is dead', but 'all that is dead'.

9 **Ch'io veda** subjunctive expressing a wish: 'May I see'. Also in lines 15, 21, 27.

11 **la mura** (archaic) = *il muro*, boundary wall.

12 **valerïane** Red Valerian (*Centranthus ruber*) is often found growing in or on old walls.

14 **ebbre** a transferred epithet; it is the poet who is 'beside himself with weeping'.

20 Pascoli is troubled by the thought that his dead relatives claim his constant affection (*vogliono ch'ami*) and want him to join them (*che vada*).

21f **quel bianco/di strada** 'the white road' to the cemetery.

26 **involale al volo** Etymological word-play is an ancient rhetorical device and may sometimes be no more than a piece of self-conscious stylistic ornamentation. Sympathetic readers will judge the present instance to be genuinely expressive: the repetition *-vola-, volo* heightens the emotive force of the noun and emphasizes the violence of the effort required to control the instinctive movements of the heart.

29 **cui presso** = *presso a cui*. Cf. **52.**41.

56. Il brivido (1903)

Pascoli's use of the refrain as an expressive device is well illustrated by this poem about death as an unfathomable and incommunicable experience. The heart of the poem is in the unanswered questions posed at the end of each stanza. *Senari* in stanzas of six lines, the last of which is printed as two separate *trisillabi* in order to isolate the refrain: $ABABXy_3-x_3$.

Title 'Il brivido che qualche volta ci scuote all'improvviso è interpretato in Romagna come il passaggio della morte'(Pascoli).

1 **corse** used transitively in the sense of *percorse*, 'ran through'.

4 **rezzo** 'chillness'; cf. Dante, *Inferno*, xxxii.75 ('e io tremava nell'eterno rezzo'), where it refers to the region of eternal darkness and cold.

7 **Com'era?** 'What was it like?'

8 'A fleeting glimpse'; *vanita* = past part. of *vanire* (archaic for *svanire*) 'to fade away'.

18 **vano** 'without trace'.

22 **lei** = *la morte*.

serra: shares with *apre* the same object *gli occhi*.

25 **che** final: 'so that no one may touch him and ask him . . .'

57. La voce (1903)

The poet looks back over his life and recalls how, in times of hardship and depression, he was saved from committing suicide by the memory of his mother, whose voice he seemed to hear speaking his name in the dialect of Romagna: *Zvanî* (Giovannino). The poem is in sections, each consisting of three quatrains (with alternate rhyme) and ending with the poet's name as a kind of refrain: ABAB.CDCD.EXEX (X is a *verso tronco*). *Novenari* in trochaic rhythm alternate with *novenari* in dactyloanapaestic rhythm. As in No. **56** the refrain plays a major part in sustaining the emotional intensity of the poem.

4 'trembling with anxiety'.

5 **una accorsa anelante** 'a woman breathless from running'.

8 A macabre touch, not uncharacteristic of Pascoli. Cf. lines 26 and 68; also **53**.72.

12 **Zvanî** The sibilant sound of the initial consonant completes the alliterative effect of the line, experienced (thanks to the word *soffio*) as a quiet whisper. The soft, plaintive effect of the refrain is assisted by the prolonged final vowel (which has to fill two metrical syllables, since this is a *verso tronco*) and by the unincisive nature of the fricative -*v*- and the nasal -*n*-. It is possible, too, that the resemblance in sound between *Zvanî* and *svaní* may contribute at an unconscious level to the emotive power of the refrain.

15 **che** may be taken either as causal ('because') or as temporal (repeating the sense of *Quando* in line 13).

18 **Reno** the river which flows through the outskirts of Bologna. Pascoli alludes to his days as a university student.

20 **Si beve?** 'Will you drink?' An invitation to the poet to drown himself.

26 **amari bocconi** a deliberate ambiguity: *bocconi* can refer back either to line 15 (in which case *terra* = 'the world') or to the mouth of the mother *piena di terra*. Cf. note on **53**.72 and on line 8 above.

27 **capiva** See note on **2**.3.

32 **ridille!** = *ridi'* (imperative of *ridire*) + *le* (i.e. *le devozioni*).

33—5 The last syllable of line 33 must be elided with the first of line 34, and the last syllable of *angelo* belongs to the following line, which otherwise is a syllable short. The rhyme is between *piange-* and *ange-*. Line 33 remains hypermetric.

38 **(nel carcere!)** a reference to Pascoli's incarceration in 1879.

che: 'when'; repeated in lines 41 and 45.

NOTES 171

50 **poi** after death.
52 **noi** the poet's mother and father, his brothers Giacomo and Luigi, and his sister Margherita.
56 **le bimbe che l'hanno saputo** refers to Ida and Maria, who had been told of their brother's arrest.
59f The victim is in his grave, but his murderer is still alive.
62 **cupi abbandoni** 'sombre moments of despair'.
72 **che** 'when'. Also in lines 73, 77.
76 **un tepore di pianto** 'warm tears'.
77 **lessi** past historic of *leggere*.

58. *Il sonnellino* (1903)

The poem describes a blissful state between sleeping and waking, when complete contentment seems to lie within reach. Woken by a thunderclap to the reality of the day, the poet feels that something infinitely precious has slipped from his grasp. Quatrains with alternate rhyme: ABAb. The longer lines are *novenari* with a dactylo-anapaestic rhythm; the short fourth line is either a senario (stanzas 1, 3, 5, 7) or a *trisillabo* (stanzas 2, 4, 6, 8).

1 **di tra** 'amid'.
7 **per tutto** = *dappertutto* 'everywhere'.
11f **e non che non fosse/silenzio** 'and yet all was silence' (literally 'not that there was not . . .')
27 By itself the line is hypermetric. The last syllable of *folgore* must be elided with the vowel at the beginning of the next line; the rhyme is between *volgo* and *folgo-*.
30 **piaciuta** 'enjoyed'.
tra il sonno 'whilst sleeping'.

59. *Il gelsomino notturno* (1901)

Gelsomino notturno is the popular name for the plant known to botanists as *Mirabilis jalapa*, the Marvel of Peru. Like other members of the family *Nyctaginaceae*, it opens and gives out its fragrance during the hours of darkness. In the garden at nightfall the petals of the 'nocturnal flowers' open; meanwhile the occupants of the house turn on the lights; later they go upstairs to bed. The poem — a kind of epithalamium — was written to honour the marriage of a friend: Gabriele Briganti.

Quatrains composed of *novenari* with alternate rhyme. The first two lines of each stanza have a dactylo-anapaestic rhythm, the second two a trochaic–dactylic rhythm.

2 **a' miei cari** Cf. 5.12, **57**.52.

14 **prese** 'occupied'.

15 **La Chioccetta** literally, 'the Hen'. It is the name given by country people to the constellation of the Pleiades (Pascoli's own note).

16 **pigolío** literally, 'chirping'; here used figuratively of the twinkling of the stars in the constellation, likened to a brood of chickens in the 'farmyard' of the sky; an example of synaesthesia.

21 Hypermetric. There is synaloepha between the last syllable of *petali* and *un* at the start of line 22. The rhyme is between *peta-* and *segreta*.

22 **si cova** 'is maturing'.

23 **urna** the 'receptacle' of the flower in which the fertilized seeds will mature.

24 'a kind of strange new happiness'.

60. La canzone del girarrosto (1901)

In Pascoli's view even the humdrum aspects of domestic life are legitimate and fruitful subjects for the poet, and some of his earliest poems bear witness to the extraordinary fascination that simple household chores held for him. The success of the present poem is due largely to its vein of lighthearted humour. Metre: four equal sections, each of four quatrains with alternate rhyme; the lines are *novenari* except for the *trisillabi* that occupy lines 2 and 4 of the third quatrain in each section. The regular dactylo-anapaestic rhythm keeps the poem moving at a brisk pace, which is momentarily increased still further by an ingenious use of *sdrucciolo* words at the end of lines 4, 8, 20, 24 and 63.

2 **sospira** because the holiday is nearly over.

3 **Che ha** Cf. **1**.1 and note.

teglia shallow pan of copper or earthenware.

4 Hypermetric, but there is synaloepha between the last syllable of *brontola* and the vowel that begins the next line. The rhyme is between *tramonto* and *bronto-*. Cf. **58**.27.

8 Cf. line 4 and note. The rhyme is between *spigo* and *sfrigo-*.

NOTES 173

11 **trovasi** = *si trova*. The inversion is for metrical convenience.

adorna 'dressed up', 'in her Sunday clothes'.

16 **giaggiolo** The reference is to the scent worn by the housewife. Orris-powder (the powdered rizomes of certain species of iris) is used in perfumes.

20 See note on line 4.

21 **parte** 'starts'.

22 **intrigo** literally, 'complexity', referring to the mechanism of the automatic spit, which is operated by clockwork. Translate: 'mechanism'.

24 See note on line 4.

27 **eguale** 'regular'.

32 **fermo** = *fermato*.

35 **scoppi** 'plops'.

37 **svolo** = *volo* 'flight', 'flying'. The forms *svolo, -are* are now obsolete.

37—40 The rapid enumeration of sounds continues without a verb.

41 **ciocchi** the logs of the fire in front of which the joint is roasting.

41f **senz'ira/né pena** 'uncomplaining, effortlessly'.

47 **nel mentre che** = *mentre*.

49 **ch'è l'ora** 'because it is time (for lunch)'.

50 The rotation of the spit (*vertigine*) may have become faster, but it is still smooth and quiet (*molle*).

57—60 The striking of church clocks announces that it is lunch-time.

63 See note on line 4. The rhyme is between *schiavo* and *tavo-*.

in tavola! 'Dinner's ready!'

64 A final comic touch: the bell attached to the automatic spit adds its shrill warning to the booming of the bells in lines 57, 59.

61. L'ora di Barga (1900)

The setting for this poem is the Tuscan village of Castelvecchio di Barga in the foothills of the Apennines above Lucca, where Pascoli went to live in 1895. The village is in the Serchio valley below Barga, whence the chimes of the clock drift down at regular intervals. To the poet they sound like a summons and a warning: that it is time to rejoin his loved ones . . . in the world beyond. Six-line stanzas rhyming ABABCC. Each line is a *doppio quinario* (two five-syllable lines joined together) as is most plainly seen in lines 7, 24, 29 and 41. The monotonous effect produced by this metre is augmented by the use of repetition and assonance.

1f **non sento/se non** 'I can hear nothing except . . .'

6 **che persuade** 'persuasive'. Pronounce as *persüade* (four syllables). Also in line 40.

11 **cose ch'han molti secoli** 'things that are many centuries old'.

21 **tinnulo** (archaic) 'tinkling'.

25 **ritorno** On its first appearance the notion of 'returning' suggests no more than a return to the house as evening closes in; the more solemn implication — death — is reserved for the end of the poem.

28 **mi traluce** The pronoun is in the oblique case: 'on me'.

33f **se c'è . . ./s'io trovi** '(to see) whether there is still . . . and whether I can find . . .' In prose one would expect the verb of both clauses to be in the same mood.

41 **ritorniamo** Cf. *ritorno* in line 25.

42 **quelli** a reference to the poet's loved ones now dead.

62. *La mia sera* (1900)

A peaceful poem expressing a mood of quiet resignation as evening falls. The ending is somewhat similar to the close of *L'ora di Barga*: darkness and sleep may be interpreted as metaphors for death. Eight-line stanzas with alternate rhyme: ABABCXCx. Except for the last line of each stanza, which is a *senario* ending with the word *sera*, the lines are *novenari* with a dactylo-anapaestic movement.

19 By itself the line is hypermetric, but the last syllable of *restano* must be read as the first syllable of line 20 to make up the deficiency in that line. The rhyme is between *tempesta* and *resta-*.

24 **nell'ultima sera** 'in the late evening'.

27f The clamour of the swallows as they fly about in search of insects (*la garrula cena*) is longer than usual: the inclement weather has made it a bad day for catching food (*povero giorno*) and they are unusually hungry.

29f **Nidi** refers to the young birds who have not yet left the nest. They have not received from the parent birds the whole of their share of food for the day (*la parte . . . intera*), meagre though that share is (*sì piccola*).

ebbero: Cf. note on **43**.13f.

31 **Né io . . .** a vague allusion to a feeling of dissatisfaction or disillusionment on the part of the poet; however, the feeling is allowed only momentarily to interrupt the prevailing mood of contentment.

33–5 Note the absolute regularity with which the word *Dormi!* is repeated, suggesting the regular tolling of a bell. For the metrical irregularities in lines 34 and 35, see the note on lines 19f. The rhyme is between *sussurra-* and *azzurra*.

37 **canti di culla** 'cradle-songs', 'lullabies'.

39 **sentivo** 'I used to hear'. The poem ends on a nostalgic note with a recollection of childhood.

40 **sul far della sera** 'at nightfall'.

63. La servetta di monte (1903)

In content the poem has a certain resemblance to No. **6** (*La cucitrice*) and No. **37** (*Con gli angioli*). The servant-girl is another of those solitary Pascolian figures who watch and wait, wrapt in their own impenetrable worlds of thoughts and feelings, dreams and memories. The isolation of the girl in this poem is heightened by the detailed description of her environment, which is quite extraneous to the inner reality of the girl herself. She remains totally abstracted, watching but not seeing. Six-line stanzas composed of *novenari* (mostly with trochaic rhythm) rhyming ABABCC.

2 **sola e selvaggia** The girl is sitting up, waiting for her employers to return home. The adjective *selvaggia* (= 'untutored', 'inexpert') may echo Dante, *Purgatorio*, ii.52f, where it is applied to people disorientated in a strange environment.

4 **staggia** a rack or horizontal piece of wood attached to the wall, with hooks from which to hang pots and pans.

5 **Fa un giro con gli occhi** 'She looks all round the room'; *giro* literally = 'circuit'.

6 **pannello** 'apron' (Pascoli's own gloss).

7 She is a newcomer to the household: a young girl who has left her mountain village to enter domestic service. Everything in her new home is still strange.

13 **musino** diminutive form of *muso*.

16   **sonaglio** 'bubble'. Pascoli's note mentions a local superstition in and around Barga: 'qui, quando la pentola fa i *sonagli*, dicono che "passano i miccetti [= donkeys]" '.

25   **È anco** = *C'è ancora*.

27ff   In her imagination the girl follows with nostalgia the mule as it climbs the hill towards the mountain village where she used to live. Perhaps the mule itself is imaginary and has come into her mind by association with the bubbles of line 16.

41f   **alla squilla/. . . della tottavilla**   The trilling of the meadow-lark (*tottavilla*) is likened to an angelus-bell (*squilla*) calling the faithful to their early-morning devotions.

64. *La cavalla storna* (1903)

The grey mare of the title refers to the horse that was bringing Ruggero Pascoli home on the day he was killed. The poet's mother, obsessed with discovering the identity of her husband's murderer, has her suspicions confirmed by the mare herself. In this dramatic narrative Pascoli handles the powerful emotional content without the mawkishness which mars other poems of his on the same theme. *Endecasillabi* in rhyming couplets.

1   **la Torre**   name of the Torlonia estate of which Ruggero Pascoli was bailiff.

2   **Rio Salto**   See the introductory note to No. 8.

3   **cavalli normanni**   See note on 24.5.

4   **frangean**   'were munching'.

9   **da essa**   'beside her', 'with her'.

10   **sommessa**   refers to her manner of speaking: 'in a low voice', 'softly'.

13   **il suo cenno e il suo detto**   each movement (*cenno*) and word of command (*detto*) by which the driver controlled the horse.

29   **lasso**   'slack'.

30   Almost a repetition of line 28. Though terrified, the mare did not show her fear by any outward sign: her heart beat quicker, but her legs did not move any faster. Literally, 'you contained your running within your racing heart'.

32   **facesse**: subject = 'he' (Ruggero Pascoli).

40   **il fuoco delle vampe**   the spurts of flame from the gun.

59   **vuote**   'hollow'.

60   **il rullo delle ruote**   'the rolling of wheels'.

62   **alto**   'loudly'.

65. *La tessitrice* (1897)

This is one of nine poems comprising the section of *Canti di Castelvecchio* entitled 'Il ritorno a San Mauro'. The girl whom the poet loves, and who is depicted as weaving her own shroud, is no longer alive except in his memory, but this revelation is reserved for the end of the poem, whose biographical origins lie partly in Pascoli's love for Erminia Tognacci. The poet himself foresaw with wry amusement that future exegetes, misled by the false notion that every lyric is a chapter of autobiography, would cudgel their brains to identify the girl in the poem and be blind to its more general significance. 'Quando non ci sarò piú io', he told his sister, 'vedrai quanto strologheranno per sapere chi poteva essere questa tessitrice, ma ti assicuro che non ne ho in mente di preciso nessuna e che le personifico in una tutte.' Alternating four-line and three-line stanzas linked by rhyme: ABAa:CBC. The poem is rounded off by a final quatrain with alternate rhyme. The fourth line of stanzas 1, 3 and 5 is a *quinario* and repeats the second half of the opening line of the stanza. Elsewhere the *doppio quinario* is used.

9 **mio bene** 'my love'.

12f **la cassa/tira del muto pettine a sé** 'she draws towards her the batten with its silent reed'. The batten or beater of a hand-loom is the swinging frame (*cassa*) that carries the reed (*pettine*). The reed consists of a number of vertical wires set close together at precise intervals between two horizontal rods; it is used for spacing the warp threads and for beating up the weft. As each new thread is laid across the warp, it must be pressed firmly in position against the already completed fabric. This process of beating up is carried out by means of the swinging batten with its reed, which the weaver in the poem pulls towards her.

16 **l'arguto pettine** Cf. 35.5 and note.

POEMI CONVIVIALI

Classical antiquity provided Pascoli with the subject-matter of the poems in this collection. His protagonists are either legendary heroes (as in No. **67**, *Il sonno di Odisseo*, taken from the group of Homeric poems), mythological figures (e.g. Silenus,

Narcissus, Psyche) or historical personages (e.g. Hesiod, Solon, Socrates, Alexander the Great). These last are portrayed with little regard for historical veracity, being presented in episodes entirely of the poet's own invention and transformed by his modern sensibility, attitudes and preoccupations. Descriptive details, on the other hand, are rendered with accuracy and precision, as may be seen in *Solon* (No. **66**), which is typical of the way in which the poems combine historical reconstruction of ambience with an individual interpretation of the subject-matter. Pascoli's subjective treatment of his materials distinguishes these poems from the *Poèmes antiques* of the Parnassian Leconte de Lisle, with which they have been compared. The overall design of the two collections is also quite different. The intention behind the ordering of the *Poemi conviviali* is to trace the evolution of values, attitudes and beliefs in the classical world from the dawn of Hellenic civilization to the advent of Christianity, and the Christian gospel is represented as the culminating point of this development in a way that would have been wholly repugnant to the anti-Christian French poet.

66. *Solon* (1895)

Solon, the celebrated Athenian statesman and poet, died in the middle of the sixth century B.C. He is represented here as sitting at the dinner-table listening to a singer from Eresos on the island of Lesbos, the birthplace of the lyric poet Sappho. The theme of the first song is love, but Solon mistakes it for the second song about death. This coupling of love and death had become almost a commonplace in the Romantic poetry of the nineteenth century, but the familiar material acquires a new lease of life in the novel setting devised for it by Pascoli in this poem, which occupies the first place in the collection. A celebration of the power of lyric poetry, it serves as a kind of preface to the volume as a whole. The narrative parts are in *endecasillabi sciolti*; the songs are in Sapphic stanzas composed (unlike the Sapphics of No. **11**) in accordance with the system of equivalences that Pascoli elaborated in his *Regole di metrica neoclassica* (see Introduction). The rhythmic patterns are:

> *endecasillabi* ′ ∪ ′ ∪ | ′ ∪ ∪ | ′ ∪ ′ ∪
> *quinari* ′ ∪ ∪ | ′ ∪

2 **votivo oro di doni** 'votive offerings of gold'.

5ff Construe: 'nulla è piú bello che udire ... e dire ... o ... godere ...'

9 **cratere** the mixing-bowl ('crater') in which wine was mixed with water before being served.

11 **dire** 'to hold forth', 'to declaim'.

13 **querulo, che piange** describing the plaintive sound of the flute.

16-27 Solon is addressed by a member of his household, who begins by quoting an elegiac couplet written by Solon himself. A literal version of the original Greek is: 'Happy is he who has dear children and solid-hoofed horses and hounds and a foreign guest-friend'.

17 **solidunghi** = *di solida unghia* (cf. line 21), imitating the Homeric epithet used by Solon; *solida* in the sense of 'uncloven', 'entire'.

18 **cani da preda** 'hunting dogs', 'hounds'.
un ospite: 'a hospitable friend' in the sense of Latin *hospes* and Greek ξένος.

23 Not quite the same as *il vino piú vecchio e il canto piú novello*; rather 'You praise the wine the older it is ...'

24 **al Pireo** 'at Piraeus'; the most important of the harbours of Athens.

26 **giunsero** 'have arrived'. Cf. note on **43**.13.

28 **Phoco** The Greek-sounding name is part of the historical colouring. It is not the name of any known person.

29f **le Anthesterïe** The Anthesteria (festival of flowers) was celebrated at Athens in the spring in honour of Dionysus, the wine-god. The wine-jars were ceremonially opened and the new wine tasted.

30 **il fumeo doglio** 'the smoke-stained wine-jars', brought from the smoke-chamber where the wine matured.

32 **l'Egeo** the Aegean sea, to the east of the Greek peninsula.

38 **pèctide** the small lyre (πηκτίς) which Sappho is reputed to have introduced from Lydia.

39 **còllabi** the pegs of the lyre to which are attached the ends of the strings. The singer is described as tightening the strings (*strinse ... le corde*) by turning the pegs of her instrument, which she is supporting (*reggendo*) with her other hand.

41ff The opening stanzas of the song (lines 41-8) draw on material from three fragments of poetry by Sappho, but the pastiche then develops in a manner quite unlike any surviving lyric by the Greek poetess.

42 **un tremolio d'argento** 'a shimmer of silver'.

46 **gèttasi** For the inversion cf. **60**.11 and note.

47 **corre** transitive; cf. **56**.1 and note.

49 **ricciute chiome** 'curly hair'; the plural is unusual.
M'è lontano The unexpressed subject is the singer's beloved.

54 **lui** her beloved, her 'sun'.

62 **ospite** 'host', but with the same associations that the word has in lines 18, 19.

64 **Togli il pianto** 'Stop weeping'.
È colpa! 'It is wrong to weep'; *colpa* = fault.

64ff The second 'Sapphic' song is entirely Pascoli's invention and bears no resemblance to any surviving poem by Sappho.

65 **Chi dirà che fui?** 'Who shall ever say that I am dead?' (literally, 'that I was once alive'): a classicizing turn of phrase. The rhetorical question is answered as the song progresses: the poet will never die as long as there are singers to sing his songs.

66 **Piangi** imperative.

68 **cocchio** 'chariot'.

70 **Rhodòpi** Rhodopis was a celebrated Greek *hetaera* ransomed from slavery by Sappho's brother, who had made her his mistress; under the name 'Doricha', she is mentioned in a lyric fragment by Sappho.

73 **apre il candor dell'ale** 'opens its white wings'; a classicizing trope.

76f **diano le rosee dita/pace al peplo** literally 'let rosy fingers leave the peplos in peace'. The peplos was a long flowing over-garment worn by Greek women. If the wearer were in mourning, her fingers would be rending her clothes.

81 **in quella** = *in quell'ora* 'at once'.

82f 'his eyes will once more look upon Sappho the beautiful, all roses'.

67. Il sonno di Odisseo (1899)

This poem is one of several of the *Poemi conviviali* inspired by the Homeric epics. It is a pastiche based on an episode in Book 10 of the *Odyssey*, where the hero, a guest of the Phaeacian king Alcinous, is recounting the adventures that have befallen him on his homeward journey from Troy. He tells of his hospitable reception in the kingdom of Aeolus, keeper of the

NOTES   181

winds; then of how Aeolus sent him on his way again with a fair west wind to blow his ship towards Ithaca and with the gift of a leather bag in which all the other winds were shut up: ' "For nine days we sailed, night and day alike; on the tenth our native soil was already appearing, and in fact from near at hand we saw people tending their fires. Then sweet sleep came over me in my weariness, because it was I who controlled the sail — I did not give the sheet to anyone else among my companions — so that we might reach our native land more quickly. But my companions talked to each other and said that I was taking home gold and silver, gifts from Aeolus" ' (28—36). ' "So they spoke, and the wicked design of my companions triumphed: they untied the bag, and all the winds rushed out. The gale immediately snatched them and carried them screaming to the open sea away from their native land. I woke up . . . and lay in the ship. But the ships were carried by a wicked gale of wind back to the island of Aeolus" ' (46—9, 53—5). It was to be another nine years before Odysseus eventually got home to Ithaca.

Pascoli develops the element of pathos latent in the Homeric narrative, describing in some detail the familiar sights and landmarks of Odysseus's homeland, which the hero glimpses only indistinctly as he wakes to find his ship heading for the open sea and Ithaca fast receding in the distance. All the salient features of this description have been culled from one part of the *Odyssey* or another (mainly from Books 13, 14 and 24), and the Italian poet has gone some way towards suggesting the language of his source, using epithets and phraseology reminiscent of Homeric style: *l'incavata nave*, (*parole*) *simili a freccie, parole simili ad uccelli* (cf. 'winged words'), *il ben cerchiato fonte, il divino mandriano, la soave opra del miele, l'eccelsa casa*. Repetitions are also used in imitation of epic style. *Endecasillabi sciolti*.

1   **e . . . e** 'both . . . and'. Also in line 7.

4   **scotte** 'sheets': the ropes attached to the lower corners of sails for regulating their tension.

6   **patria** 'homeland'; see note on the title of No. **4**.

18   The passage of time in the poem is marked by changes in the word beginning the last line of each section.

22   **ella prendea del cielo** 'it touched the sky'.

23   **i bótri** the gullies down which the mountain streams could be seen falling in 'foaming' cascades (*spumeggiando*).

27 **la nuova erba del grano** the fresh young corn-shoots.

28–30 The description paraphrases *Odyssey*, xiii.242f, 246.

35 **già** emphatic; also in line 53.

36 **notando** from *nuotare*.

37–9 The crew are discussing in whispers the possible contents of the mysterious leather bags (*otri*) of line 75.

40f The rock of Corax (= raven) and the spring Arethusa are named in *Odyssey*, xiii.407f as the place where Eumaeus the swineherd kept Odysseus's pigs.

41 **ben cerchiato** literally, 'well-girt', i.e. encircled by a strong wall.

43–50 The description follows *Odyssey*, xiv.5–12.

46 **divino** translates Homer's δῖος: 'excellent', 'noble'.

53 **Eumeo** Eumaeus.

55 **da prua . . . a poppa** 'from stem to stern'.

57 **fremiti** The voices are now quivering with passion.

58 **Forkyne** The harbour of Phorcys, named in *Odyssey*, xiii.96.

59–63 Cf. *Odyssey*, xiii.102–6: 'At the harbour's head there is a slender-leafed olive tree, and near it a lovely spray-filled cave, the holy place of the nymphs who are called water-sprites. Inside there are mixing-bowls and pitchers of stone, and there too the bees store their honey.'

63 **la soave opra del miele** 'honey, the sweet product of their labour'.

66 **acquosi** literally, 'damp' (the alders are growing near water, as alders do), but the epithet is ornamental rather than genuinely descriptive.

69 **trama** 'web'.

70 **ricrescea** 'was growing again'. Every night Odysseus's wife undid some of the previous day's work so as to delay the completion of the weaving and the moment when she must carry out her promise of marrying one of the importunate suitors.

74 **il peggio vinse** i.e. the argument amongst the companions of Odysseus ended with their deciding to open the bags (*otri*) containing the winds.

75 **la furia . . . dei venti** 'the violent winds'; cf. note on **66.73**.
ne 'from them'.

77 **peplo** See note on **66.76f**.

78 **inasprire** 'to dry hard'.
79 **lontanò** = *si allontanò* 'departed', 'sailed away'. Cf. **45**.56.
80 **un giovinetto** The boy is Telemachus, the ten-year-old son of Odysseus. See line 117.
83 **un veloce cane** Odysseus's dog Argos. See lines 89, 120.
85 **volte** 'circling', 'running in circles'.
87 **orme** 'tracks', i.e. the wake of the ship.
93 **Laerte** Odysseus's old father Laertes, the previous king of Ithaca, was still alive when the hero finally reached home.
95–100 The details are taken from *Odyssey*, xxiv.336–41.
96 **tuttavia fanciullo** 'although he was still a child'.
97f **questo ... quello** Understand *albero* in each case.
105 'screwing up his tired eyes against the light'. The first sense of *limare* is 'to file down, make sharp or thin'; here it is used of the action of half-closing the eyes so that only a narrow beam of light can enter.
122 **già percorreva** It was early morning (see line 17), but Penelope was already seated at her loom, her hands moving across it (*percorreva*) as she worked.
123 **vide non sapea che nero** 'he saw something black'.

POEMI ITALICI

68. Paulo Ucello (1903)

The name of the Florentine artist Paolo Uccello (1397–1475) is chiefly associated with the development of perspective drawing, which he pioneered. Good examples of his painting technique can be seen in London's National Gallery ('The Rout of San Romano') and in the Ashmolean Museum at Oxford ('A Hunt in a Forest'). How and when Paolo di Dono acquired the name Uccello is uncertain, though Vasari, in his life of the artist, asserts that it was a nickname alluding to the painter's love of birds. Pascoli adopts this suggestion and portrays the artist as a simple-hearted man imbued with a Franciscan love of all created things and of birds in particular. From Vasari Pascoli took a number of circumstantial details about the life of Uccello, as for example that he decorated his home with paintings of birds, cats and dogs, and other animals which he was too poor to own as pets.

Pascoli the philologist is as much in evidence in this poem as in *Solon* and *Il sonno di Odisseo*. The division of the poem into *capitoli*, each with a rubric summarizing the contents of the chapter, follows a medieval format exemplified by one of the most celebrated works in the whole literature of Christian hagiology: *I fioretti di san Francesco*, written by an unknown author in the fourteenth century. By this device the renaissance painter is brought into association with the medieval saint, to whom − according to Pascoli − he was devoted, but there is no historical evidence for this. The archaic syntax and vocabulary of the chapter-headings faithfully reproduce the language of the *Fioretti*. The verse, too, is characterized by a generous dosage of archaic words and word-forms taken from the *Fioretti* and contemporary sources, and this archaizing process combines with the habitual simplicity of Pascoli's verse syntax to produce a poetic idiom of indeterminate remoteness. The title itself is an archaic spelling of Uccello's name, one of the forms used by the artist himself in signing his work. *Terza rima*.

CAPITOLO I

Rubric: **in prima** 'in the first place'.
dipintore old form of *pittore*.

2 **mazzocchio** a circlet or coronet such as may surmount a heraldic coat of arms; see Vasari's life of Uccello, which mentions this exercise in the perspective drawing of *mazzocchi a punte a quadri tirati in prospettiva per diverse vedute* ('circlets with square studs drawn in perspective from various angles').

3 **scortava** 'was painting in perspective'; *scortare* is a painting term: 'to foreshorten'.

4 **nell'occhio** in his mind's eye.

5 **che** temporal: 'when'.
Donatello the Florentine sculptor (1386−1466), a friend of Uccello.

6 **ser Filippo** another friend: Brunelleschi (1377−1446), architect of the dome on Florence cathedral. The title *ser* was an old Tuscan title of respect usually reserved for lawyers and ecclesiastics.
era ristato a crocchio 'he had stayed chatting';
crocchio = a small group of people.

7 **fringuello** used in the general sense of 'finch' and referring to the bullfinch described in lines 8−10.

12 **lo comprava, se ci aveva** a colloquial alternative for *l'avrebbe comprato, se avesse avuto*.

grosso: a small silver coin in circulation at this time; a similar coin in England was called a 'groat'.

13f **arco/di porta** 'door-panel', 'tympanum': the space over the door, between lintel and arch.

14 **San Tomaso** Vasari mentions a painting of the saint by Uccello 'above the door of the church of St Thomas in the Mercato Vecchio'.

gli avveniva impersonal construction: 'he chanced to say'.

15 **È un fraticino di San Marco** San Marco was the Dominican monastery at Florence. The conspicuous black markings of the bullfinch put the painter in mind of the habit worn by Dominican monks, the Blackfriars.

CAPITOLO II

Rubric: **stanzuola** 'room' (not very large).

24 **pini ... nere** parasol pines.

28 **al pero** 'on the pear-tree'.

30 **sur** = *su* the addition of *-r* prevents elision with the first syllable of *una*.

bruna bruna repetition of the adjective gives it superlative force.

acqua di polle 'spring'.

31 **a cuori** 'heart-shaped'.

32 **a grado a grado** 'gradually'.

35 **lenti** 'pliant'; an archaism.

36 **lunghi** tall and thin.

41–4 allude to the painter's use of perspective.

CAPITOLO III

Rubric: Archaisms are much in evidence: **essa** (from Latin *ipsa*) = *quella*; **d'ogni sorta uccelli** = *uccelli di tutte le specie*; **in vederli** = *nel v.*; **averli non poteva** (inverted word order).

59 **calavi** 'swooped down'.

CAPITOLO IV

Rubric: **creature** = 'creations', 'things created', as in the famous poem by St Francis, variously known as the *Laudes creaturarum*, *Cantico delle creature* and *Cantico del sole*.

67 **Poi che** 'When'. The temporal use of this conjunction is archaic.

senza né ... né 'without either ... or'.

68 **anche** Construe with *ciuffolotto*: 'the bullfinch as well'.

70 **fatto motto** = *parlato*. The idiom is antiquated except in its negative uses.

72 **Giotto** (1266/7–1337): the great Florentine painter, the architect of the cathedral bell-tower at Florence.

74 **terzïarïo** A 'tertiary' is a lay-person who lives under the guidance of and in harmony with the spirit of a religious order (in this case the Franciscan order). The word derives from the term *terzo ordine* (Third Order) and distinguishes lay-associates, who had taken no vows, from fully professed men and women (monks and nuns) in the First and Second Orders respectively.

76f **il saluto/dell'angelo** 'Ave Maria', Gabriel's words of greeting to Mary when he came to announce the future birth of Christ (cf. Luke, i.28).

78 **vivuola** an old form of *viola* = 'viol'.
leuto: an old spelling of *liuto* = 'lute'.

79 **silvestra** = *silvestre*, i.e. full of the scent of wild flowers.

80 **persa** 'sweet marjoram' (*Origanum maiorana*).
uliva 'smelt sweet'.

81 **giuncava** 'strewed', 'covered'. Pascoli adapts and extends the meaning of *giuncare* (literally 'to put rushes down on the ground'), perhaps with Spanish broom (*Spartium junceum*) in mind.

83 **ser Brunellesco** See note on line 6.

84 **garzoni** used in the old sense of 'young bachelors'.

86 **Santa Maria del fiore** Florence cathedral.

CAPITOLO V

Rubric: **pur** = *pure* 'also'.

89ff Uccello uses language borrowed from St Francis and his followers, who referred to the Saint's renunciation of worldly possessions as his wedding with the Lady Poverty. In the *Fioretti* both St Francis and Fra Lione are *pecorelle di Dio*.

91 **non ha** = *non ci sono*, archaic.
fanti ... fancelle old words for 'menservants ... maidservants' found in the *Fioretti*.

95 **un podere in Cafaggiolo** See Vasari's life of Donatello.

96 **Donato** Cf. line 5. The artist's full name was Donato di Nicolò di Betto de' Bardi.

98f The implication is that, for the person who has grown it, even a simple plant like garlic is a unique (*singolar*) source of satisfaction.

100 **bene** 'wealth', 'possessions'.

NOTES 187

in iscórto 'in perspective' (cf. note on line 3). The prosthetic *i-* is for euphony and metrical convenience.

101 **a secco** on dry plaster, as distinct from the technique of painting on fresh plaster before it has dried out.

102f **sono ... in mercato** 'I'm worth as much as an egg-vendor in the market after all'.

106 **di buono** 'really and truly'.

107 **picchi** plural of *picchio* 'woodpecker'.

108 **che ci sia, non che ci paia** '(one) that will really be there and not just appear to be there'.

CAPITOLO VI

113 **il fi di Pietro Bernardone** Saint Francis; *fi* = old form of *figlio*.

114 **Ecco e** The pleonastic *e* marking the start of the main clause is a not uncommon feature of early Italian prose.

119 **cattivello** The diminutive ending softens the reproach and expresses affection. In the *Fioretti* terms like *cattivello, poverello, omicciuolo, pecorella* are frequently applied by St Francis to himself and others.

125 Archaic vocabulary: *verga* = 'stick', 'staff'; *calzamenti* = 'shoes and stockings'; *tasca* = 'purse' or 'scrip'; cf. Matthew, x.9-10, paraphrased in *Fioretti*, Cap. 2.

126 **foresti** 'wild'; another archaism.

128 **disïare** archaic = *desiderare* 'desire'.

130 **sirocchia** archaic = *sorella*. The application of the terms 'sister' and 'brother' to animals and even to inanimate objects is found in the *Fioretti* and derives from the *Cantico del sole* by St Francis.

CAPITOLO VII

Rubric: **desío** archaic = *desiderio*.

ei = *egli*.

tanto 'a great deal'.

136 'All he could feel there was a fluttering'.

137 **Onde** causal: 'Wherefore'.

138 **poverel di Dio** See note on line 119.

139 **desii** 'desire'; cf. line 128.

140 **prigione** 'prisoner'; an archaism.

142 **E'** = *Egli*.

Mugnone a stream running into the Arno near Florence that gives its name to a district famous for its woods: setting of the famous Calandrino story by Boccaccio (*Decameron*, VIII, 3).

143 **Galluzzo** a village on the outskirts of Florence, existing in Dante's time (see *Paradiso*, xvi.53).
mendico 'poor', 'needy'.

149 **laudi** *Laudi* or *laude* (singular *laude* or *lauda*) were songs in praise of God or the saints sung by members of lay confraternities in the Middle Ages.

151 **frati minori** a pun: literally, *frati minori* = 'smaller brethren' (the birds); in ecclesiastical terms the expression = 'Friars Minor', the Franciscan order.

153f St Francis alludes of course to nests (*celluzze*) and to the open countryside (*chiostro*).

CAPITOLO VIII

161 **Ne lagrimò** 'He wept to see it'.

166 **di sua mano** 'with his own hand'.

CAPITOLO IX

177 **lontanando** = *allontanandosi*. Cf. **45**.56.

178 **a mo' di** 'in the manner of'; *mo'* is an apocopated form of *modo*.
pio: implies 'conscientious', 'devoted to his task'; cf. **27**.19.
brice: plural of *bricia* ('crumb'), an obsolete form ousted by the diminutive *briciola*.

183 **sgrollo** (dialect) = *scrollo* 'shaking'.

185 **Scattò** normally intransitive.

188 **Greccio** a village in Umbria, where there is now a famous Franciscan monastery founded not long after the death of St Francis; not inconceivably the scene of the episode recounted in *Fioretti*, cap. 22, the taming of the wild turtle-doves.

189–94 The description may have been inspired by a famous episode in the *Fioretti* telling how St Francis preached to the birds.

189 **verziere** 'orchard'; an archaism.

195 **sminuiva** = *si sminuiva* 'he was getting smaller'.

196 **cinque stelline** the stigmata of the saint, which continue to be visible as points of light ('little stars') even though the rest of him is now too far away to be discernible. Cf. *Fioretti*, cap. 26: 'le sue cinque istimate erano siccome cinque stelle bellissime'.

197 **bruscinar** (dialect) = *piovigginare* ('drizzle'), used to suggest the pitter-patter of raindrops.

198 **un trito becchettío sonoro** 'the sound of the pecking

of countless little beaks'; *trito* = 'frequent'; *becchettio* = *becchettare*, from *becchetto* 'a little beak'.

CAPITOLO X

Rubric: **addormito** = *addormentato*.

201 **ito** past part. of *ire* 'to go'; here preferred to *andato* for its sound (imitating the song of the nightingale).

202 **Ne stormí** *Ne* = 'From there', i.e. from the bush (also in lines 203f). The subject of this and following verbs is the nightingale, whose song accompanies the other sounds of nature.

206 **ne** = *di lui*, referring to the vanished saint; also in lines 207f.

ODI E INNI

Not all the poems in this collection celebrate heroic deeds or momentous happenings. All are characterized by gravity of tone and an elevated style, but whereas the 'Hymns' are frequently inspired by important public events or resound with nationalistic fervour, the 'Odes' contain many poems of a more personal and reflective nature like Nos. **69–71** in the selection. Neoclassical metres figure prominently throughout. Those used in the *Odi* derive from Horace; in contrast, many of the *Inni* imitate the rhapsodic style of the choral odes of Pindar.

69. A una morta (1907)

An unusual kind of 'In memoriam' poem, whose starting point is the humanistic affirmation that the dead woman here commemorated — her identity is unknown — lives on in the thoughts of the poet. This nucleus is developed through several stages and a succession of different emotions: apprehension (as the poet remembers that he himself must die), reassurance (stemming from a hope that the soul may be immortal) and finally anguish (at the thought of his disembodied soul deprived of the physical means of expressing his feelings). With the title *L'anima* and with slightly different versions of lines 5, 6, 13 and 20, the poem appeared in the first edition of *Odi e Inni* (1906). Six quatrains, linked in pairs by the rhyme-scheme (ABBC;ADDC), produce three sections corresponding to the stages of development of the theme. *Settenari* throughout, the last line of each quatrain being a *verso tronco*.

3f   The aromatic resin of certain trees is one of the materials from which incense is made.

5   **vivi, vivi** best taken as imperative, though the indicative also makes sense.

10   **Ch'io creda** 'Let me believe' (in the immortality of the soul). The three subjunctives that follow express three more desires.

12   The syntax is elliptical, but the meaning is clear: the poet hopes that the soul (*anima*) and the capacity for thought (*pensiero*) will not be subject to death (*servi*) in the same way as the physical body (*vene e nervi*).

19f   **quando.../cerchi** 'Whenever it searches' or 'if it should search'.

21   **quando ... voglia** the same construction as the above.

70. *Il cane notturno* (1899)

The poem, which evokes a nocturnal landscape and the quiet of a sleeping household, is not dissimilar in content from poems in the collections *Myricae* and *Canti di Castelvecchio*. Metrically, however, its affinities are with the rest of the Odes. In each quatrain lines 1 and 2 are unrhymed and consist of a *quinario piano* followed by a *quinario sdrucciolo*; lines 3 and 4 form a rhyming couplet and are both *novenari* with dactylo-anapaestic rhythm. The scheme is only slightly different from the one used by Carducci for the Alcaic stanzas of *Odi barbare* (e.g. in *Alla stazione in una mattina d'autunno*).

1   **Nell'alta notte** Cf. 46.43, 52.71.
tra: 'amid'; also in lines 2, 18, 21.

1f   **sento ... sento; trilli ... grilli** The use of assonance and alliteration is widespread in the first five stanzas (cf. lines 7f, 9f, 17); the effect is suggestive of the echoing of sounds in the stillness of the night.

2   **múrmure** (poetic) = *mormorío*.

3   **piovoso** swollen by the rain.
Serchio Pascoli's home at Castelvecchio was in the valley of the Serchio. See introductory note to No. **61**.

7   **sonare** depends on *sento* (line 2).

15   **alterno** 'alternating' can refer either to the sound (tick-tock) or to the movement of the pendulum of the clock.

17   **Va! Va!**   The imperatives are chosen to imitate the sound of barking.
20   **che sembra che ascolti**   'which seems to be listening'; *sembra* is impersonal.
21   **chiuse le palpebre**   absolute construction.
23   **letto di foglie**   The simple mattress is a bag filled with leaves.
25. **nella zana di vetrici**   'in her wicker cradle'.
27   **S'inseguono**   The reflexive pronoun has reciprocal force: 'chase one another'; also in lines 32, 34.
28   **uguali**   'regular'.
35   **sul fare del giorno**   'at daybreak'.
36   **ritorno**   the return to consciousness.

71. *L'isola dei poeti* (1899)

The three poets celebrated in the poem are: (1) the author of the *Odyssey*, for whose Sicilian origins cf. Robert Graves, *The Greek Myths*, section *170.1*; (2) Theocritus (*c.* 300–*c.* 260 B.C.), a native of Syracuse, who established pastoral poetry as a distinct literary genre; (3) Stesichorus of Himera (fl. 600 B.C.), author of choral lyrics admired for their dignity and grandeur. In conception and style the poem bears a family resemblance to the neo-classical fantasies (the *Primavere elleniche*) in Carducci's *Rime nuove*, especially the second, the 'Dorica': 'Sai tu l'isola bella . . .?' etc. There, as here, Sicily is the setting for a celebration of the genius of early Greek poetry as interpreted by the Romantic imagination. Sapphic stanzas, as No. **11**; the regular, almost monotonous movement of the verse is due to the preponderance of *endecasillabi* with heavy stresses on the 4th and 6th syllables.

1   **Il treno andava**   Pascoli is on a train travelling down the Italian peninsula towards the straits of Messina.
1f   Construe: 'la brezza mi pungea gli occhi'; the night is not yet over, and a fresh wind blows from the darkness of the distant straits and beyond (*tra quella . . . ombra lontana*), as yet unknown to him (*ignota*).
7   **uguale**   'unchanging' and so 'monotonous'.
7f   **il sonno . . . l'uscio**   The personification of sleep has a strong classical flavour.
molli: literally, 'loose', i.e. 'smooth', 'well-oiled'.
uscio: the door of consciousness.

9   **di là d'esso** 'beyond it', 'on the other side of it'.
11 **uguale** 'regular'; cf. line 7.
12 **tetracordo** 'tetrachord', a four-stringed instrument.
13 **alcuno** the poet of the *Odyssey*.
14 See introductory note to No. **43** and cf. *Odyssey*, xii.39−54, 166−200.

17−21 See *Odyssey*, xii.127−41, 260−9. After passing the Sirens and escaping the dangers of Scylla and Charybdis, Odysseus and his companions reached Thrinacia (Sicily), 'the island of the Sun', where they found the herds and flocks of Helios tended by the 'long-robed goddesses' Phaethusa and Lampetie.

20 **armentarie** 'shepherdesses'.
21 **con grandi pepli** paraphrases the Greek word τανύπεπλος (= 'with flowing robes'); cf. note on **66**.76f.

21f The twanging of the tetrachord (which accompanied the recitation of the *epos*) gives way to the shrill sound of the shepherd's pipes, introducing the second poet, Theocritus.

33−6 The third poet, Stesichorus, is introduced by the sound of lyres (*cetre*) and flutes. The word *loto* is a transliteration of the Greek word for a flute made from the wood of the lotus-tree.

33 **Ecco e** Cf. note on **68**.114.
33f **il tintinno/dorico** 'the tinkling Dorian strain'; it was the Dorian invaders of Greece who developed the choral lyric.
35 **chiarosonante** 'clear-sounding'; a compound adjective with a dithyrambic flavour.
39 **ondoleggiando cadono giú** literally, 'swaying gently this way and that (the feathers) fall to earth'; *ondoleggiando* (an archaism) describes the gentle oscillating movement of the feathers as they fall.
42 **Etna** the still active volcano at the eastern end of the island.

piú su de' 'higher than', i.e. beyond the sight of.
47 **sorta** past part. of *sorgere*.
49 **Salve** 'Hail!'.

54−6 The modern poet wishes to be recognized as a direct descendant of the poets of antiquity, but he is uncertain whether (*in dubbio se*) he will get the welcome he desires.
55 **ospite** See note on **66**.62.
lui object of *ravvisi*.

72. *Inno degli emigrati italiani a Dante* (1911)

Dated 'Castelvecchio 1911', the poem 'was written for the colonies of Italian settlers in the United States and was to have been set to music and sung on the occasion of the inauguration of the monument to Dante in New York' (translation of Pascoli's own note). The Italian 'exiles' in America address Dante, the exile from Florence, and hail him as the prophet of the discovery of the New World by Columbus. The fact of the poem's composition reflects Pascoli's abiding concern for the plight of Italian workers in a period of mass-unemployment and mass-emigration; the poem itself, after initially striking a note of pathos with the word *Esule*, concentrates on the figure of Dante as the heroic embodiment of the genius of the Italian people. *Terza rima* (the metre of the *Divine Comedy*) articulated in three sections of ten lines each.

2   **cui** direct object of the verbs *scisse* and *spinse*.
patria Florence; Dante was exiled in 1302 and never returned to his native city.

3   **legno** 'ship' (in apposition to *cui*).

4   **scendesti ... Ulisse** alludes to Dante's imaginary journey through Hell in the first *cantica* of the *Divine Comedy* and to the encounter with Ulysses in *Inferno*, xxvi.76–142.

5   The adjectives paraphrase Greek epithets applied to the hero in the *Odyssey*: πολύτροπος (which Pascoli interprets as 'much-travelled') and πολύτλας ('much enduring').

7–10   A free paraphrase of the exhortation of Ulysses to his companions as recounted by Ulysses himself in *Inferno*, xxvi.112–20.

7   **l'occidente** used, as in *Inferno*, xxvi.113, to mean 'the western extremity' of the known world, which the ancients identified with the straits of Gibraltar; here Hercules erected two pillars (one in Africa, the other in Spain) to mark the utmost limits of legitimate travel (*ibid*.99f); beyond lay the waters of Ocean and the uninhabited regions of the world (*il mondo senza gente*).

8   **prima** adjective: 'early'.
altrui 'for other people'.

9   **nel mondo senza gente** taken over from *Inferno*, xxvi.117.

10   **giovera** = *piacerà* 'it will be pleasing'; archaic, Latinizing use of *giovare*.

11 **l'Oceano** the Atlantic, the beginning of the 'stream of Ocean' which, according to Greek mythology, flowed round the world.

insonne 'unresting'.

12 **uno** Columbus, who obtained from Ferdinand and Isabella in Granada the money he needed to finance his voyage of discovery.

12f **sulle porte/schiuse e vietate** 'on the threshold of the open but forbidden gates' (the pillars of Hercules).

14 **pose** past definite of *porre*.

a segno 'as a mark'; see note on line 7.

14f **che in sorte/... ribelle** literally, 'who received as his lot (the) eternal (spirit of) rebellious youth'. Pascoli adapts to his own purposes the circumstance mentioned in *Odyssey*, xi.603 that Hercules, after arriving in Olympus and being made immortal, married Hebe (who was later allegorized as the goddess of youth and called by the Romans *Juventas*).

18f **sul rombo / di** 'following the course of'.

19 **caravelle** 'carvels', the Spanish sailing ships used by Columbus.

20 **adduci** 'take'. Pascoli revives the etymological meaning of *addurre* (from Latin *ad-ducere* = 'to conduct to').

23 The 'long foaming track' is a metaphor for the destiny of the Italian nation, whose ship is guided by the immortal helmsman Dante.

25 **Santa Maria** one of Columbus's ships.

27 **purpúreo** perhaps another reminiscence of the language of the Homeric epics. Cf. πορφύρεος (= 'dark-gleaming') as an epithet applied to the sea.

28 'there appeared what looked like a grey cloud'.

29 **Pinta** another of Columbus's ships.

29f The conjunction of the words *'Terra'* and *'Sí'* calls to mind *Inferno*, xxxiii.80, where Italy is called 'il bel paese là dove il *sí* suona'. With the arrival of Columbus in America a part of the New World becomes Italian.

30 **alta** 'loud'.

infinita i.e. heard by peoples all over the world.

SELECT VOCABULARY

Unless otherwise stated, nouns ending in *-o* are masculine, those ending in *-a* are feminine. Stress is indicated if it does not fall on the penultimate syllable, even when the accent does not appear in the text. Words explained in the notes are not usually included in this vocabulary, and only meanings relevant within the context of the poems are given.

abbaiare, to bark
abbandonare, to leave; (rfl.) droop, fall forwards
abbracciarsi a, to embrace
abbrividire, to quiver, shudder
abisso, abyss
àbito di sposa, wedding-dress
abituro, humble dwelling
àbside (f.), apse
acacia, acacia, wattle, mimosa
accartocciato, shrivelled
accecare, to blind
accògliere, to welcome, receive
accomodato, settled, comfortable
accorato, sorrowful
accórrere, to run up, come running
accorto, knowing
accostarsi, to approach, draw near
accostato, left ajar
acquazzone (m.), downpour, heavy shower
addío, farewell
addirsi, to be becoming
additare, to point out, to
addormito (poet.), asleep
adorare, to adore
adorno, adorned
aèreo, aerial; airy, high in the air; insubstantial
affaccendato, busy
affacciarsi, to show oneself; **a. alla finestra**, to look out of the window
affannarsi (di), to worry (about)
affanno, distress
afferrare, to grasp; **afferrarsi a**, to clutch at
affocato, red-hot, on fire
aggradare, to be pleasing
aggrandire, to grow bigger
agitare, to shake; flap (*wings*)
agnello, lamb
agonia, agony, pangs of death; **fare l'a.** to breathe one's last
agreste, rustic
aguzzo, sharp, pointed
aia, threshing-floor, farmyard
alabastro, alabaster
alato, winged
alba, dawn, daybreak
albaspina, hawthorn
albeggiare, to dawn; to show white

alberello, jar
albicocco, apricot-tree
albore (m.), (light of) dawn
alfine, finally
alga, seaweed
aliare, to flutter
alitare, to blow softly
àlito, breath; light breeze
allontanarsi, to move away
alloro, bay-tree
alluminare, to shine on
altana, roof-terrace, balcony
alterno, alternate, alternating
altri (invar. subj. pron.) another (person), someone
altrove (adv.), elsewhere
altrui (invar. pron., gen.), of another, another's
alzare, to hoist, raise
ametista, amethyst
ampio, ample, wide, spacious
ànatra, duck
ancella (poet.), maid, hand-maiden
àncora, anchor
anelante, breathless
ánfora (storage-), jar
ángiolo, *angelo* angel
ànima, spirit
ansare, to pant
antelucano (adj.), before dawn
antro, cave
apparire to appear
appressarsi, to approach
apprestare, to get ready, supply
aquilone (m.), north wind
ara, altar
arare, to plough
aratro, plough
arbuscello, *arboscello* bush
arca, coffer, chest

arcata, arch
arco, arch; bow
arcobaleno, rainbow
ardore (m.), warmth
arduo, steep; lofty
argentino, silvery
àrgine (m.), embankment
arguto, sharp, quick-witted; shrill (*sound*)
àrido, dry
arnia, beehive
aroma, -i (m.), aroma, scent
arpa, harp
arrestarsi, to stop
arrídere, to smile
arrotare, to grind smooth
artiglio, talon
ascia, adze, axe
asilo, refuge
àsino, ass, donkey
aspirare, to breathe in
aspro, rough, harsh, sharp; (fig.) fierce
assai (adv.), very
assenso, assent
assiduo, assiduous, ceaseless, untiring, regular
assiepare, to hedge
assïuolo, scops owl
assopito, drowsy, dozing
asta, staff
astrale, astral
astro, star, luminary, heavenly body
àtomo, atom
attèndere, to wait (for); a. a to listen intently to
attento, attentive, intent
attíngere, to draw
auleta (m.), flute-player
aura (poet.), air, breeze
àureo, golden

SELECT VOCABULARY

aurora, dawn
austero, austere
avello (poet.), tomb
avere a, da (+ inf.), to have to (do something)
avventare, to throw violently
avvertire, to notice
avviarsi, to set forth, go on one's way
azzeruolo, *lazzeruolo* (Neapolitan) medlar

babbo, father
badare (trans.), to take care of, look after; (intrans.) pay heed (to), listen (to)
bagnare, to steep, bathe, wet
baia, bay
balenare, to flash
baleno, flash
balza, cliff
balzare, to leap
bàratro, abyss
barbaglio, glitter
basílico, basil
bassura, lowland
bàttere, to hit, strike
batticuore (m.), heart-throb; fear
battuta, blow, knock
bearsi, to rejoice
beato, blessed, happy
beccare, to peck, pick up
becchino, grave-digger
becco, beak
bel bello (adv.), quietly, peacefully, slowly
beltà (f.), beauty
bene (m.), good, happiness
benedizione (f.), blessing
berillo, beryl

biada, fodder
biancheggiare, to be, appear, show white
biancospino, hawthorn
bifolco, ploughman
bigello, coarse grey cloth
bimba, -o, child
biricchino, young scamp
bisbigliare, to whisper
bisbiglio, whisper
blando, mild, soft, soothing, sweet, caressing
boccia, -o, -uolo, bud
boccone (m.), mouthful
bombo, bumble-bee
bonaccia, fair weather, calm sea
borbottare, to mutter, murmur
borchia, ornamental metal disk or stud
borgo, township, (small) town, (large) village
bosso, box (*tree, hedge*)
botro, gully
bove (m.), ox
brage (f.), *brace* live coal
bramare, to long for
branco, flock
brezza, breeze
briglie (f. pl.), reins
brillare, to shine, gleam, sparkle
brívido, shiver, shudder
bronco, stump
brontolare, to mutter, murmur
brónzeo, bronze (adj.)
bruco, grub, worm
brullo, bare, barren
bruma, mist
brunito, burnished
bruno, brown, dark

brusío, murmur of voices, whispering
brusire, to whisper, murmur, rustle
bruto, brute
bubbolío, rumble (of distant thunder)
bue (pl. *buoi*), ox
bufera, storm
bugno, beehive
buio, dark(ness)
busso, bússolo = *bosso*

cadenzato, rhythmical
calandra, (calandra) lark
calare, to fall, swoop down
càlcola, treadle (*loom*)
càlice (m.), calyx
calígine (f.), thick fog, darkness
calma, stillness
calpestare, to trample on
calura, heat
camerata, dormitory
camino, fire-place
campanile (m.), steeple, belfry
campano, -accio, bell (for animals)
camposanto, cemetery
cancello, gate
càndido, white
candore (m.), whiteness
canna, pipe; (pl.) reed-pipes, shepherd's pipe
canoro, singing (adj.)
cantatrice (f.), singer
càntico, canticle, hymn, song
cantilena, song, monotonous chanting
canto, song
canto, -one, -uccio, corner
cantore (m.), singer
cantuccio, corner, nook
canuto, white-haired
canzone (f.), song
capanna, hut, hovel, shack
capannello, small group, knot of people
capinera, black-cap (*bird*)
capo, head; end
capodaglio, bulb of garlic
cappuccio, hood, cowl
capra, goat
càrcere (m.), prison
càrdine (m.), hinge
carrettiere (m.), wagoner, carter
carta, leaf of a book
cascare, to fall
cascata, waterfall
casolare, (m.) (poor) cottage, simple country dwelling
casto, chaste
catena, chain
cateratta, sluice
cattivo, nasty; naughty
cauto, cautious
cavo, hollow; deep
cèdere, to yield, give up, hand over
cedro, cedar
celare, to conceal
cella, cell
celluzza, little cell
cémbalo, cymbal
cennamella, bagpipe
cennare, *accennare* to point (to)
cenno, sign, gesture
ceppo, log
cèreo, waxen, very pale
cerúleo, sky-blue
cetra, lyre
ché, because, for

SELECT VOCABULARY

checché (indef. pron.), whatever
chiacchiericcio, chattering (n.)
chiarità, brightness, effulgence, glow
chiaro, brightness, light
chiassoso, noisy
chiazza, stain, spot
chicco, grain; berry (one of a bunch)
chino, bent, bowed (*head*), lowered (*eyes*)
chiòcciola, snail
chioccolare, to whistle (like a bird)
chioma, head of hair, tresses
chiostro, cloister
chiuso (*chiudere*, p.p.), enclosed, shut up
chiuso (n.), enclosure (for animals)
cianciare, to chatter
ciarliero, loquacious, talkative
cicala, cicada
cicaleccio, chattering (n.)
ciglio (pl. *le ciglia*), eyelash
cigno, swan
cigolare, to squeak, creak
cilestrino, light blue, sky-blue
ciliegio, cherry-tree
cima, top
cinabro, vermilion
cincia, tit
cíngolo, cincture, girdle
cinguettío, chirping, twittering (n.)
ciocca, see **viola a ciocca**
ciocco, log
cirro, cirrus (*cloud*)
ciuffo, tuft
ciuffolotto, bullfinch
codesto, this here

collare (m.), collar
colle (m.), hill
colmo, brimful
colombo, dove
colonna, pillar, column
colorarsi, to assume a colour
colpettino, tap
comando, command
compassione (f.), compassion, pity
compianto, lament
composto, composed, serene
comprèndere, to understand
confine (m.), boundary
conforto, consolation
confuso, indistinct
congiúngere, to join, clasp
consolare, to comfort, cheer
contare, to count
contorto, twisted
convento, monastery
convito, banquet
coppa, goblet
coppia, couple, pair
coppo, oil-jar
cor(e) = *cuore*
corazza, cuirass, breast-plate
corda, string (*musical instrument*)
cornacchia, crow
cornamusa, bagpipe
corona, rosary; crown; garland
córrere (trans.), to run, travel through
corvo, crow
cosí come, just as
cosmo, cosmos, universe
costellazione (f.), constellation
costí (adv.), there
cotale (adj.), such
covata, brood (*chickens, etc.*)

cratere (m.), crater, mixing-bowl (for wine)
crèdulo, credulous; **c. di** ready to believe in
crepa, crack, crevice
crepitare, to crackle; rustle (*paper, leaves*)
crèpito, crackle
crepuscolare, crepuscular, of (the) dusk, twilight (adj.)
cresta, crest
criniera, (horse's) mane
cristallo, crystal
crocchio, group (of people); **stare a c.** to chat together
croccolío, gurgling noise
croce (f.), **in c.** crossed, folded
crocitare, *crocidare* to caw, croak
crollo, collapse; jolt
crosta, husk
cruccio, irritation, anger
cucitrice (f.), seamstress
cuculo, cuckoo
culla, cradle
cullare, to cradle, rock, lull
culto, *cólto* cultivated
cuna, cradle
cuore (m.), heart
cupo, dark, deep; hollow
cúpola, dome
curare, to pay heed to

daccanto (adv.), close at hand
dardo, arrow, dart
deh!, alas!
desco, table (for meals)
deserto, solitary
desío (poet.), longing
destare, to rouse, stir, wake
dettare, to dictate
detto, word

deviare, to turn aside
devozioni (f. pl.), prayers
dí (m., invar., poet.), day
digradare, to get progressively smaller
dileguare, to fade away, dissolve, melt away, disperse, disappear, vanish
dilungarsi, to move away
diradarsi, to dissolve
dirómpersi, to break up, disintegrate
dirupo, rocky cliff
discórrere, to talk
disfatto, torn apart
disparte: in d., some way away
disperare, to despair
disteso (*distendere*, p.p.), spread out
distínguere, to distinguish
distògliere, to divert, turn elsewhere
dito, finger
divieto, prohibition
dòcile, docile, obedient
doglia, pain
dolere, to be painful
dolersi, to be sorry
dolore (m.), sorrow, pain
donare, to bestow, give
donde (adv.), from where
dondolare, dondolarsi, to rock, sway
dondolío, swinging (n.)
dóndolo, rocking motion
dono, gift
doppio (n.), peal of bells; **sonare a d.** to ring the full peal
dorare, to gild
drago, dragon
dubitoso, uncertain

SELECT VOCABULARY

e' (pron.) = *ei, egli*
ebbro, drunk; (fig.) delirious, beside oneself
eccelso, lofty
echeggiare, to echo, resound
eco (m., f.), echo
èdera, ivy
educanda, girl at a convent school
effóndere, to emit, give out
Egeo, Aegean sea
emèrgere, emerge, issue (forth)
emigrato, emigrant
émpiere, empire, to fill, invade
erba: far e., to cut grass (for fodder)
erboso, grassy
eremitaggio, hermitage
eròe (m.), hero
errare, to wander, roam
erta, (upward) slope, steep path; all'e. (adv.) on the alert
esalare, to exhale, breathe forth
esclamare, to exclaim
èsile, slender
esplorare, to scrutinize, examine
èssere (m.), being, existence
esterrefatto, terrified
estínguere, to extinguish; (rfl.) die
èsule (m., f.), exile; (adj.) exiled, in exile

faccenda, business; in faccende busy, doing a roaring trade
faggio, beech-tree
falasco, grass (used in straw-plaiting)
falce (f.), sickle, scythe
falciare, to mow
fanale (m.), lantern; f. di fortuna storm lantern
fanciullezza, childhood
fardello, bundle; pack; burden
fascia, band
fascio, bundle (of sticks); beam of light
faticato, *affaticato* tired
favilla, spark
femminile, feminine, of women
fèndere, to cleave
fermento, ferment
fèrreo, iron (adj.), metallic
fèrtile, fruitful
festa, rejoicing
festivo, festive, holiday (adj.)
fiammeggiare, to blaze
fiammella, little flame
fianco, flank, side
fico, fig-tree
fidarsi, to trust
fido, faithful, trusty
fieno, hay
fiero, proud; intrepid
fiévole, feeble; faint (*sound*)
fifa, peewit
fíggere, to fix
filare (trans.), to spin; (intr.) to drip, trickle; speed onwards
filare (m.), row (of trees, vines)
filigrana, filigree-work
filo (pl. -i, m., -a, f.), thread, wire
fimo, manure
fine, senza f. endlessly
fino, fine, pure (unadulterated)
fioccare, to fall in flakes
fiocco, tassel; tuft (of wool)

fioco, faint (*sound*)
fiorire, to flower
fiorita, efflorescence, (a quantity of) flowers
fiorito, flowering, in bloom; **f. di** adorned with
fiottare, to wave, undulate
firmamento, firmament, heavens
fischiare, to whistle
fischiettare, to whistle softly
fischio, whistling
fiso, steady, firm
fissare, to gaze at
fisso, fixed
fiutare, to sniff
flagellare, to lash, scourge
flauto, flute
flòrido, flourishing, vigorous; buxom; floriferous, free-flowering
fluire, to flow
foce (f.), (river-) mouth
focolare (m.), fireside, hearth
fogliame (m.), foliage
fola, fable, tale
folgorare, to shine, flash
fólgore (f.), lightning flash
folto, dense, close-set, lush, thick
fóndere, to melt
fondo, deep
fonte (m.), spring (*water*)
forapaglie (m. invar.), warbler
forestiero, stranger
fornello, stove
forra, ravine, gorge
forziere (m.), coffer, chest
fosco, dark, gloomy
fossa, ditch
fossato, brook
fràgile, fragile, brittle, delicate

fràgola, strawberry
fragore, roar, crash, clatter, clanking, noise
frana, landslide
franare, to collapse
fràngere, to break, crush
frasca, bough
frastuono, din
frate, brother (monk)
fratta, thicket, brake, clump of brambles, bushes
freccia, arrow, shaft
fremebondo, quivering
frèmere, to quiver
frèmito, quiver
fringuello, finch, chaffinch
frogia, nostril (*animals*)
fronda, leafy branch, leaf
fronte: a f. a f., face to face
fronzuto, leafy
frufrú (m.), rustling; (fig.) turmoil
frugare, to rummage, search
frullare, to flutter, whirr
frullo, flutter
frumento, corn
frúscio, rustling
fuga, flight
fugace, fleeting
fuggévole, fleeting
fúlgido, shining
fumare, to smoke
fúmido, steaming, smoking, smoky
fúnebre, funereal, funeral (adj.)
furia, rage, violence
fuso, spindle (for spinning)

gabbiano, sea-gull
galla, oak-apple
gallo, cock

SELECT VOCABULARY

galoppare, to gallop
galoppo, galloping (n.)
gambo, stalk
gàrrulo, garrulous, clamorous, chattering
gelsomino, jasmine
gèmere, to lament, moan, groan
gèmitò, moan
gemma, bud
gemmare, to bud
gesto, gesture
ghiaia, shingle
ghiandaia, jay
già (adv.), formerly, once
giaggiolo, iris (*flower*)
gialleggiare, to appear yellowish, turn yellow
giglio, lily
ginepro, juniper
ginestra, broom (*plant*)
giocondo, merry, gay
giogo, yoke; (mountain-) ridge, peak
gioire, to rejoice
giovare, to avail, be of service
girarrosto, turnspit, roasting-jack
giuncaia, reed-bed
glauco, glaucous, grey-green
glútine (m.), gluten, glue
gobbo, bent
gocciare, to drip, trickle
godere (intrans.) to be glad; **g. di** to enjoy, delight in
gómito, elbow
gorgogliare, to gurgle
governare, to steer
governo, government
gracidare, to caw
gràcile, slender, delicate
grano, wheat, corn; grain (of sand, corn, etc.); bead (of rosary)
gràppolo, bunch, cluster
grata, grating, grille
grave, heavy, deep, solemn, grave
gregge (m.), flock; pl. *le greggi*
greggia, flock
grembo, womb; lap
gremire, to fill (up)
gremito, crowded (with)
greppia, crib, manger
greto, (dry gravel-) bed of river or stream
greve, heavy
grido, cry; pl. *le grida, i gridi*
grillo, cricket
gronda, gutter
grotta, cave
gru (f.), crane
grufolare, to root about (*pigs*)
gualcito, crumpled
guazza, heavy dew
guazzare, to splash about, wallow
gufo, owl
guidare, to guide
guizzare, to dart, glide
guizzo, flash
guscio, skin (*fruit*); husk, shell (*nut*)

ignaro, unaware, unknowing; **i. di** ignorant of
ignorare, not to know, to be ignorant of
ignorato, unknown
ignoto, unknown, uncharted
ignudo, naked
imbrunare (poet.), to grow dark
immèrgere, to immerse

immòbile, unmoving
immobilmente, without moving
immortale, immortal
immoto, still, motionless
impalpàbile, impalpable, intangible
impaziente, impatient
impero, command
implorare, to implore
imprímere, to imprint
improvviso, unexpected, sudden
inalzare, *innalzare* to raise
incamminarsi, to set out
incantamento, incanto, spell
incarnarsi, to become incarnate
incavato, hollow
incenso, incense
incominciare, to begin
incorare, to encourage
incurvarsi, to curve
indifferente, uninterested
inebriare, to intoxicate
inerte, lazy
infame, infamous
infermo, sick
infinito (adj.), infinite, boundless, numberless, endless; (n.), the infinite
infornare, to put in the oven
infuso, infused
inginocchiarsi, to kneel
inginocchiato, kneeling
ingombro, weighed down; heavy, overcast (*sky*)
ingrassare, to grow fat
inno, hymn
inoltrarsi, to advance
inquieto, restless, uneasy
inseguire, to pursue, chase after

inserire, to insert
insístere, to insist
insonne, sleepless, wakeful
intanto, meanwhile; **in tanto che** whilst
interminàbile, endless
interminato (poet.), boundless
interrogare, to question
intrecciare, to plait
intrídere, to knead
invisíbile, invisible
invitato, guest
invito, invitation
invogliarsi di, to conceive a desire for
involare, to steal, carry off; (rfl.) steal away
ira, anger
iroso, irate, angry
irraggiare, to irradiate, shine on
irrequieto, restless
irsuto, shaggy, bristly, prickly
irto, prickly, thorny
issare, to hoist (*sails*)
istante (m.), instant

lacca, lacquer
lagrimare, to weep
lamento, lament, cry of pain
lampo, flash of lightning
lànguido, languid
languire, to languish
larva, ghost
lasso, tired, weary; slack
làstrico, paving, paved surface
latrare, to bark
latrato, bark
lavandara, *lavandaia* washerwoman
leggío, book-rest, reading-desk
leprotto, leveret, young hare

SELECT VOCABULARY

lettino, little bed, cot
levarsi, to rise, arise
libeccio, south-west wind
lichene (m.), lichen
lido, beach, (sea)shore
lieto, merry
lieve, slight; soft (*sound*)
lilla (m., invar.), lilac
limitare (m.), threshold
límpido, limpid, clear
lino, linen
liscio, smooth
litanía, litany
lívido, livid, the colour of lead
lodare, to praise
lòdola, (sky-)lark
loglio, darnel (a weed)
luccicare, to gleam, glitter, glisten
lúcciola, fire-fly
lucente, shining
lucerna, oil-lamp
lúcido, shining, bright
lúgubre, mournful
luí (m., invar.), warbler (*Phylloscopus*); l. piccolo, chiffchaff
lume (m.), light, lamp
lunge, lungi (adv.), far away
lupinella, sainfoin
lustrare (trans.), to polish; (intrans.) shine
lutto, mourning (n.)

macchia, scrub, thicket, *maquis*
màcchina, apparatus
madreselva, honeysuckle
maestra, school-mistress
maestrale, cold (N.W.) wind
maggese (f.), fallow field

mago, magician
maiale (m.), pig
malato, sick
male (m.), illness; evil, harm
màndorlo, almond-tree
mandra, herd, flock
mandriano, herdsman
mannella, sheaf of corn
mano: a m. a m., gradually
mantello, mantle
marcito, rotting
mareggiare, to swell, surge (*sea*)
marina, seashore
marinaio, sailor
marra, mattock, hoe
marruca, Christ-thorn
massaia, housewife
masso, boulder
matassa, skein; tangle
mattinale, morning (adj.)
mattutino, morning (adj.)
maturare, to mature, ripen
medicina, medicine
meditare, to ponder, plan
melo, apple-tree
melograno, pomegranate-tree
mèmore, mindful
menare, to lead
mendico, beggar
mensa, (dining-) table
menta, mint
meridiano, noonday (adj.)
meriggio, noon
merlo, blackbird
messe (f.), crop
mesto, sad, sorrowful
metro, measure (*rhythm*)
mezzo (adv.), half
mezzodí (m., invar.), noon
mica, crumb
midolla, pith

miele (m.), honey
migrare, to migrate
miràbile, wonderful
mirare, to gaze at, watch
misto a, mingled with
modesto, modest
molle, soft
molleggiare, to spring about
monachino, bullfinch
monastero, convent
mondo (adj.), clean, pure, unsullied
monòtono, monotonous
montano, mountain (adj.)
monte (m.), mount, mountain
mora, (fruit of *m. selvatica*) blackberry
mormorare, to whisper, murmur
mormorazione (f.), grumbling, complaining
mormorío, murmuring
moro, mulberry-bush
morso, bite; bit (*bridle*)
mortale, mortal
moto, motion, movement, agitation
mucca, (dairy-) cow
mucchio, pile, heap
muco, mucus
mugghiare, to howl (*wind*), roar (*wind, sea*)
muggire, to howl (*wind*)
muletto, young mule
muòversi, to move, stir
mura, *muro* wall
muraglia, (high) wall
múrmure (m., poet.), murmur
muso, nose (*animal*)
mutare, to change
muto, silent

nastro, ribbon, band
nativo, native
nebbione (m.), fog, heavy mist
nebbioso, misty, foggy
nembo, cloud; (poet.) cloudburst, squall
nemico, hostile
nereggiare, to appear black
nervo, nerve, sinew
nettare, to clean
netto, distinct, clear
nevoso, snow-covered
nido, nest; nestlings
nitrito, neigh(-ing)
niuno (pron.), no one
nodo, knot
nota, note
noto, well-known, familiar
notturno, nocturnal
novella, story
novello, new
nube (f.), cloud
nulla (m.), nothing
nunzio, messenger
nuove (f. pl.), news
nutrice (f.), nourisher

oblío, oblivion, forgetfulness
odorare, to smell (sweet)
odorato di, fragrant with
odorino, faint smell
odoroso, fragrant
olezzare, to be fragrant, smell sweet
olivo, olive-tree
olmo, elm-tree
oltre (prep., adv.), beyond
oltremarino (adj.), from overseas
ombrella, umbel; parasol
ondata, wave

SELECT VOCABULARY

ondeggiante, undulating
ontano, alder
ora (adv.): **ad o. ad o.**, now and again, from time to time
orfano, orphan
oriuolo, clock
orlo, edge, verge
orma, mark, track, footprint
ormai (adv.), by now
ornello, manna- (or flowering) ash
orto, orchard, garden
orzo, barley
oscillare, to oscillate, sway about, swing to and fro
oscuro, obscure; dark, murky, gloomy
òspite (m., f.), guest
osso, bone
osteria, inn
otre (m.), leather bag, container
ottuso, blunt
ove, *dove* where
ozio, laziness
ozioso, lazy, indolent

padiglione (m.), tent, canopy
padule (m.), marsh
paese (m.), country; village
paglia, straw
pago, content, satisfied
palafreno, palfrey
pàllido, pale
pàlmite (m.), shoot
palo, stake, (telegraph-) pole
pàlpebra, eyelid
palpitare, to tremble, quiver
pàlpito, tremor, pulsation, throb
pàmpano, vine-leaf

panchetta, (short) bench
panico, millet, bird-seed
panno, cloth
paranzella, fishing boat
parco, frugal
pari (invar. adj.), like
parte (f.), share, portion; **da p.** on one side
parvenza, appearance
pàscere (trans.), to feed, feed on, pasture; (intrans.) graze
pàscolo, food
passaggio, crossing
passare (intrans.), to pass off, cease (*pain*, etc.); (trans.) pass, cross
passeggero (adj.), fleeting; (n.) passer-by
passo, step, footfall; passage
pastore (m.), shepherd
pastura, pasturage
paziente, patient
peccare, to sin
pece (f.), pitch
pecorella, lamb, (small) sheep
pellegrino, pilgrim
pendice (f.), slope, hillside
pèndulo, dangling, hanging
pennacchio, plume
pennello, paint-brush
pensoso, thoughtful, pensive
penzolare, to hang (down), dangle
perché (m., invar.), reason, cause
percórrere (trans.), to traverse
percuòtere, to strike
perenne, perennial, never-failing
pèrgola, pergola, arbour
perla, pearl
pero, pear-tree

perpètuo, constant
persino (adv.), even
persuadere, to persuade
pertinace, persistent, pertinacious
pervenire a, to reach
pesco, peach-tree
pésta, footstep
pètalo, petal
petto, bosom
pezzo (*time*), quite a while
pezzuolo, morsel
piagare, to wound
pianeta, -i (m.), planet
piano, flat, smooth, level; **pian piano** (adv.) (very) slowly; softly, quietly
pianta, plant, tree
pianto, tears, weeping, lament (-ation), sorrow
picchio, knock, tap; woodpecker
piccino, little, little boy
picco, (mountain-) peak, crag
piena, spate, flood
pieve (f.), parish church
pigolío, chirping (n.)
pio, devout; compassionate, tender
piombare, to plumb
piombo: a p., vertically (down)
pioppo, poplar-tree
piovano, parish priest
píppolo, grain; pip, stone (*fruit*)
plàcido, placid, serene, peaceful
plaudire, to applaud
plenilunio, full moon
poco: a p. a p., little by little
podere (m.), farm, estate

poema (m.), (long) poem, epic
poggiato, leaning
poggio, hillock, knoll, small hill
polare, polar
polla, spring (*water*)
polledro, *puledro* colt, foal
pòlline (m.), pollen
polveroso, dusty
pometo, (apple-) orchard
pomo, fruit
poppa, stern (*ship*)
pòrgere, to offer, hold out
pòrpora, purple
porre, to place, put, lay down
pòrtico, portico; (pl.) colonnade
posa, pause, rest
posare, to rest; (rfl.) perch
posta, stall (for horse)
potare, to prune
povertà, poverty
pratería, meadows
preda, prey
prèmere, to press
presso (prep.), near, beside; (adv.) nearby
prillare, to twirl
procella (poet.), storm(-wind)
profeta (m.), prophet
profondità, depth
profondo, deep
profumare, to scent
profumo, scent
prolungare, to prolong
prora, bow(s) (of ship)
prorómpere, to break out, burst forth
prospettiva, perspective
prua, bows (of ship)
prunalbo, hawthorn

SELECT VOCABULARY

puffino, puffin
pugna (poet.), struggle
pulsare (trans.), to strike, play (*musical instrument*); (intrans.) throb, pulsate
punta, tip; headland
punto: **in p.**, ready, prepared
pupilla, pupil (*eye*)
pure (adv.), also; however, nevertheless
pútrido, rotten

quadro (adj.), square
quaglia, quail
quale, like, just as
quando: **a q. a q.**, from time to time, now and then
quarzo, quartz
quasi (adv.), as it were, like; almost
quegli (m. sing. pron.), he, that one
quercia, oak-tree
quèrulo, querulous, complaining
queto, *quieto* quiet, peaceful
quiete (f.), peace, quiet

raccògliere, to gather
ràdere, to graze; (fig.) to pass close to, skirt
ràdica, root
rado, infrequent, occasional
radunare, to gather, bring together
raganella, tree-frog
raggiare, to radiate
raggio, ray (*light, sunshine*)
raggiúngere, to catch up with
ragionare, to talk, discourse
ragnatelo, cobweb
rama, *ramo* branch

rame (m.), copper; (pl.) (copper) pans, cooking utensils
rampollare (da), to emerge, arise (from, out of)
ramuscello, *ramoscello* twig
ranella, little frog
ràntolo, wheezing
rapito, enraptured
raro, rare, occasional
rasente (prep.), very near
raso, satin
raspare, to scrape, scratch (about)
rauco, hoarse
ravvisare, to recognize
recare, to bring, carry
recídere, to cut off
rèduce (adj.), returning, come back
regamo, wild marjoram
règgere, to support, hold (up), control
remoto, distant
rena, sand
rèndere, to yield, produce
reo, evil, wicked
rèquie(m) (m.), requiem, prayer for the dead
resta, beard of corn
retaggio, heritage
rete (f.), (hair-) net
retta: **dar r.**, listen, pay attention
retto, straight
rezzo, shade
rialzare, to raise again
riascéndere, to mount again
ribrezzo, shudder
ricciuto, curly
ricercare, to look for
ricetto, shelter, refuge

209

richiamo, (bird-) call, song
ricinto, *recinto* surrounded
ricondurre, to bring back
ricongiúngere, to reunite
ridire, to say again, repeat, tell
rifare, to remake
riflesso, reflected
rigo, (boundary-) line
rigonfio, swollen, full
riguardare, to look again (at); stare at
rilúcere, to shine
rimasticare, to chew the cud
rimbalzare, to rebound
rimbombare, to resound, boom, thunder, roar
rimbrottare, to rebuke
rimirare, to see again; stare at
rimproverare, to reproach, reprimand
rincórrere, to chase after
rincréscere (impers.) to displease
rinforzare, to reinforce, strengthen
rinfranto, broken up
ringhio, snarl
rintócco, stroke (*bell, clock*)
rio, stream, brook
ripensare, to think again (about)
ripiantare, to replant
ripiegare, to bend (back)
riposo, rest, repose
riprèndere, to resume, continue (speaking)
risa (f. pl.), laughter
risacca, surf
risata, (burst of) laughter
risentire, to hear again
risonare, to echo, resound
risplèndere, to shine
rissare, to quarrel
ristare, to pause, remain
ritorno, return
ritto, standing
rivenire, to come again
rivívere, to relive
rivo, stream
rivòlgersi, to turn over, round, back
rócca, distaff
roco, hoarse, raucous
ródere, to consume, eat away, erode; (rfl.) fret, worry
rombare, to boom, resound
rombo, booming sound, humming, buzzing, beating (*wings*); (naut.) course, direction
romito, solitary
ronca, billhook, pruning-hook
rondinella, -otto, young swallow
ronzare, to hum, buzz, drone
ronzío, buzzing
rosaio, rose-bush
ròseo, roseate, rose-coloured, rosy
rosignolo, nightingale
rosseggiare, to glow red
rotolare, to roll
rovina, ruin
rovo, bramble, blackberry-bush
rubino, ruby
rugiada, dew
ruminare, to chew (the cud)
rupe (f.), crag, rock
rupestre, rocky
ruzzare, to play, romp

SELECT VOCABULARY

saggiare, *assaggiare* to taste
saggio, wise, wise man
salcio, *salice* willow
salpare, to weigh anchor
salso, salty
saluto, greeting
salvare, to save, preserve
salvàtico, *selvàtico* wild
sanguinolento, dripping blood
sano, healthy
santuario, sanctuary
saputo, knowing, wise
sasso, stone
sassoso, stony
savio, wise, wise man, sage
sbalzare, to leap (up)
sbarrare, to bar
sbàttersi, to flap
sbocciare, to blossom
sbucare, to emerge
scabro, rugged
scagliare, to hurl
scalpicciare, to shuffle one's feet
scalpiccío, tramping of feet
scalzo, barefoot, bare-footed
scarnito, emaciated
scarno, lean
scattare, to jerk, make a sudden movement
scheggia, splinter
scheletrito, reduced to a skeleton
schèletro, skeleton
schianto: di s., suddenly
schiavo, slave
schiccherare, to daub
schidione (m.), spit
schiera, rank, line; company, band, group
sciabordare, to splash
sciacquío, splashing sound, lapping, plashing

scialbo, colourless, wan
sciame (m.), swarm (*bees*, etc.), host
scíndere, to sever
sciògliere, to loose, let loose
scodinzolare, to wag the tail
scogliera, rocky foreshore
scollo, neck-hole, opening
sconosciuto, unknown
scoppiettare, to crackle
scoppio, gun-shot, explosion, peal of thunder
scordarsi, to forget
scòrgere, to descry, perceive, make out, discern
scorza, bark
scrollare, to shake
scrosciare, to roar (*water*)
scuòtere (p.p. *scosso*), to shake
sdipanare, to unwind
seccia, stubble
seco = *con sé*
seguace (adj.), following
seguitare: s. la via, to continue on one's way
selva, wood
selvaggio, wild, untamed, untutored
seme (m.), seed
semichiuso, half-closed
seminare, to sow
seminatore, sower
seno, breast
sentire, to feel, smell, hear
sentore (m.), scent, odour, smell
serenità, serenity
sereno, serene, tranquil; (n.) clear sky
serpente (m.), snake
serrare, to close
servetta, maid, young servant-girl

SELECT VOCABULARY

servo, slave
severo, austere
sfavillare, to sparkle
sfiorare, to brush past, caress, touch lightly
sfogliare, to turn over the pages of a book
sfrascare, to rustle
sfríggere, to hiss, sizzle
sfrigolare, to sizzle, sputter
sfumare, to disappear, evaporate
sgabello, stool
sgomento, dismay
sgretolato, crumbling
sgridare, to scold, rebuke
sguardo, glance, look
sibilare, to hiss, whistle
síbilo, hiss, whistle
sí e no (adv.), indistinctly
sílice (f.), silica
silvestro, wild
sincero, honest, genuine
singhiozzare, to sob
singhiozzo, sob
singolare, singular, peculiar
singulto, sob
sino a, until
sirena, siren; fog-horn
slanciato, slender
smarrire, to lose, mislay
smarrito, lost, strayed, bewildered
sminuire, to diminish
smorto, wan, washed out
snello, slender
soave, soft, gentle
soavemente, gently
soavità, sweetness
socchiuso, ajar
sodaglia, untilled ground

soffiare, to blow
soffice, soft
soffio, blowing, breath; whisper; breath, puff, gust, blast (of wind)
soggolo, wimple (nun's headdress)
soglia, doorstep, threshold
sognare, to dream (about)
solatío, sunny
solcare, to furrow, cleave
solco, track, furrow
solingo, lonely, solitary
solitario, deserted
solitúdine (f.), solitude
sommèrgere, to submerge
sommesso, quiet, subdued
sommo, top; tip (*finger*)
sonante, ringing, resounding, echoing
sonnecchiare, to doze
sonnellino, nap, short sleep
sonnolento, sleepy, drowsy
sonoro, sonorous, resonant
sordo, dull, muffled, muted
sòrgere, to get up, arise, rise (up)
sorsata, gulp, drink
sorte (f.), lot, destiny
sorto, p.p. of *sorgere*
sospèndere, to suspend, hang
sospirare, to sigh
sospiro, sigh
sostare, to pause
sotterra (adv.), underground
sovra = *sopra*
sovrano, supreme, sovereign
spalletta, parapet
spàndere, to spread (abroad)
spàrgere (p.p. *sparso*), to scatter, spread

SELECT VOCABULARY 213

sparire, to disappear
sparpagliare, to scatter, disperse
spavento, terror
spaziarsi, to soar
spennellata, brush-stroke
sperso, dispersed, scattered, lost
spesso, frequent
spianare, to roll out
spiare, to watch, look on
spiga, spike (*flowers*)
spigo, lavender
spilla, -o, pin
spina, thorn
spíngere, push, thrust, drive
spiraglio, hole, small opening
spogliare, to strip
spola, shuttle
spólvero, fine flour
sponda, bank
spossare, to weaken, deprive of strength
sprone (m.), buttress
spruzzo, spray
spruzzolare, to sprinkle
spugna, sponge
spumeggiare, to foam, froth
spuntare, to appear, emerge, peep out
squilla (angelus-) bell
squillare, to ring (out), peal, sound, chime, resound, shrill
squillo, ringing (sound)
squittire, to yelp
stagno, pond
stalla, cowshed, stall
steccato, fence
stecchito, dried up
stelo, stalk, stem
sternutare, to sneeze

stilla, drop
stillare, to drip
stipa, brushwood; (feather) grass
stoppia, stubble
stormire, to rustle
stormo, flock (of birds)
storno, (dappled) grey
straccio, shred
stradale (m.), road
strame (m.), straw
strano, strange
strepitare, to clamour
strèpito, noise, din
strídere, to whirr, make a strident noise
strídulo, shrill, strident
strillo, shriek, shrill cry
stríngersi, to draw near
strosciare, *scrosciare* to pelt (*rain*)
strúggersi, to be worn away
stuolo, band, group
stupire, to be astonished
súbito (adj.), sudden
succèdere a, to follow
succhiare, to suck
suco, *succo* juice
suolo, ground
suora, nun, sister
susino, plum-tree
sussulto, start, spasm
sussurrare, to whisper, murmur
sussurrío, whispering, murmuring
sussurro, whisper, murmur
svelare, to reveal
sverlare, to chirp
svestirsi, to get undressed
svolare, to fly
svoltare, to unfurl

tacchina, turkey(-hen)
tacitamente, silently
tàcito, silent
taglialegna (m., invar.), woodman, wood-cutter
tamerice (m.), tamarisk
tardivo, late, tardy
tardo, slow, late
tarlo, wood-worm
tastiera, keyboard
teco = *con te*
tégola, (roof-)tile
tela, linen, cloth
telaio, loom
telo, piece of cloth
tempio, temple
temporale (m.), storm
tèndere, to stretch, spread (a canopy), erect (a tent)
tenebra, (more usually *tènebre*, pl.) dark(ness)
tentare, to tempt; try, test
tentennare, to shake to and fro
tènue, tenuous, thin, slender
tenzonare, to contend
tepore (m.), warmth
terrapieno, bank, embankment
teschio, skull
tèssere, to weave
tessitrice (f.), weaver
tetro, gloomy, dark
ticchettío, ticking (noise)
timoniere (m.), helmsman
tíngere, to dye
tinnire = *tintinnare*
tino, wine-vat
tintinnare, to tinkle
tintinno, *tintinnío* tinkle, tinkling
tocco, *toccato* touched
tomba, tomb, grave

tonfo, thud
topazio, topaz
topo, mouse
toppo, log, felled tree
tórbido, cloudy, muddy
tordo, thrush
torrente (m.), mountain stream
torto, crooked
tórtola, **tórtore**, *tórtora* turtle-dove
tortura, torture
torvo, surly, ferocious
tottavilla, meadow-lark
tra, between; among, amidst
tragico, tragic
tralcio, vine branch
tralice: in t. (adv.), askance
tralúcere, to shine (through)
trama, weft, web; (fig.) pattern, design
tramontana, north wind
trànsito, passage, crossing
trapasso, death
trarre, to draw, drag
trascolorare, to change colour
trascórrere (trans.), to run, travel through; (intrans.) pass, flow past
trasparire, to show through; **t. da** to appear through
trastullarsi di, to play with
tratto: a tratti, at intervals; **a un t., d'un t.** suddenly
trave (f.), beam, rafter
trebbiatrice (f.), threshing machine
tremare, to tremble, shiver
tremendo, fearful
trèmito, trembling (n.)
tremolare, to tremble
tremolío, trembling, shimmering (n.)
tremore (m.), tremor, shaking

SELECT VOCABULARY

trèmulo, tremulous, trembling, quivering, flickering
trèpido, trembling, anxious
tribú (f.), tribe
tributo, tribute
trillare, to trill
trillo, trill
trina, lace
trito, worn, commonplace, shabby
troppo: essere di t., to be in the way
tuffare, to plunge, dip
túmido, swelling, swollen
tumulto, tumult, turmoil
túrbine (m.), gale
turbinío, whirling (movement); (fig.) confusion
turchino (adj., n.), deep blue
tuttora (adv.), still

uggiolare, to whine
uguale, uniform, unchanging, regular
ulivo, olive-tree
ululare, to howl
úlulo, howl
unghia, hoof
universo, universe
uragano, hurricane
urlare, to shout
urlo, shout, cry, howl(ing)
urna, urn
uscio, door, entrance
usignolo, nightingale
uso a, accustomed to

vacca, cow
vagabondo, vagrant
vagito, whimpering, crying (n.)
valeriana, valerian (*plant*)
vampa, flame

vanire (poet.), to fade, vanish
vano, vain, empty, fruitless, ineffectual
vapore (m.), vapour, mist, effluvium
varcare, to cross
vasto, vast, immense
veduta, sight
veglia, vigil, watch
velare, to veil, conceal
velato, (of sound) muffled, muted
veleggiare, to sail
velloso, hairy
velo, veil; (fig.) mist
vena, vein
ventata, gust of wind
verla, *averla* shrike
vermicciolo, little worm
vermiglio, vermilion
verro, boar
versare (trans.), to pour (out), shed; (intrans.) spill over
verso, song, sound (*birds, insects*)
vertígine (f.), giddiness; rotation
verzicare, to be verdant
verzura, verdure, green foliage
vespro, evening
veste (f.), dress, garment, suit of clothes; (pl.) clothes
vétrice (f.), osier
vetro, window-pane
via (adv.), away; **v. v.** gradually, successively; **per v. di** because of
viburno, viburnum
vietare, to forbid
vígile, vigilant, alert
villano, farmer, farm labourer
villoso, hairy

vinto, overcome
viola, violet; v. a ciocca, violacciocca wallflower
violàceo, violet-coloured
viottola, path
vischio, mistletoe; bird-lime
visione (f.), vision
vita, life; waist
vite (f.), vine
vívere (di), to live (on)
vociare, to shout
vocío, shouting, clamour
vòlgere, (p.p. *vòlto*) to direct, turn; (rfl.) turn round
volo, flight; a v. (adv.) in passing
voltare (trans.), to turn (over)
vòmero, ploughshare
vòrtice (m.), swirl
vuoto, void (n.)

zampa, hoof
zampillare, to spurt out
zampogna, bagpipe, reed-pipe
zana, cradle
zappa, mattock
zirlare, to sing, whistle (like a thrush)
zòccolo, hoof
zolla, clod, lump of earth